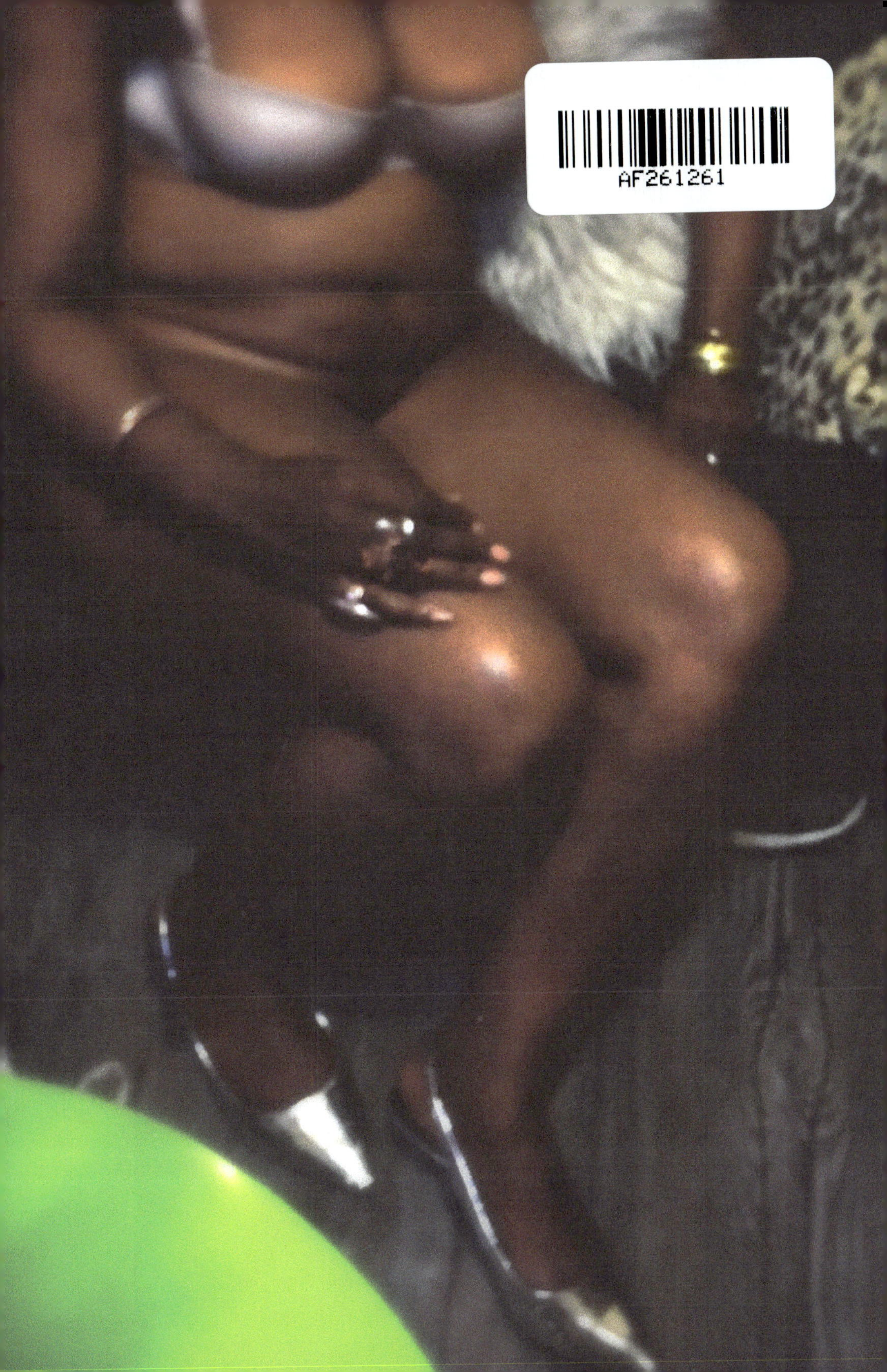
AF261261

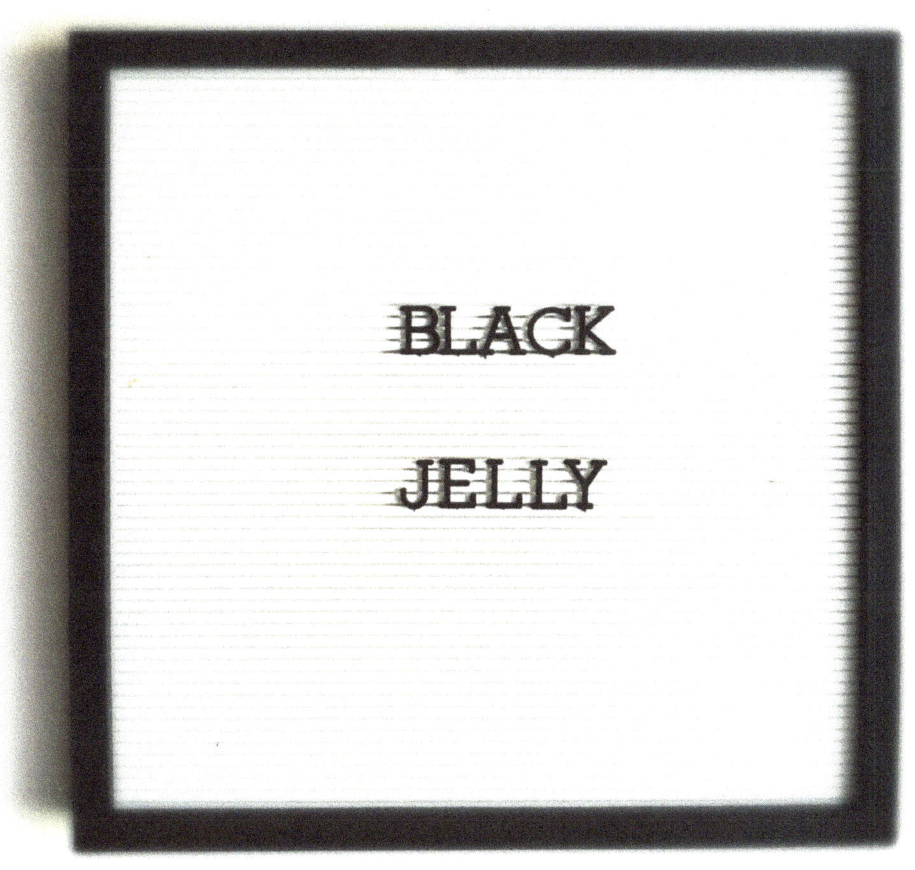

POEMS BY **MELANIE MARIA GOODREAUX**
PHOTOS BY **NIKKI JOHNSON**

FLY BY NIGHT PRESS
A SUBSIDIARY OF A GATHERING OF THE TRIBES, NEW YORK CITY, 2019

Printed in the United States of America
First Edition

Poems by Melanie Maria Goodreaux
Photos by Nikki Johnson
Cover design by Rev. Diane Sullivan
Page design by Don Eggert

Poems typeset in Asap by Pablo Cosgaya with titles set in
Averia Libre by Dan Sayers under the Open Font License

Title: "Black Jelly"
ISBN: 978-1-7321260-4-6

www.blackjellybook.com

*This book is dedicated to my sister Monica
who bakes great sweets
and is the deep, beautiful, quiet, hidden woman that lives in us all.*

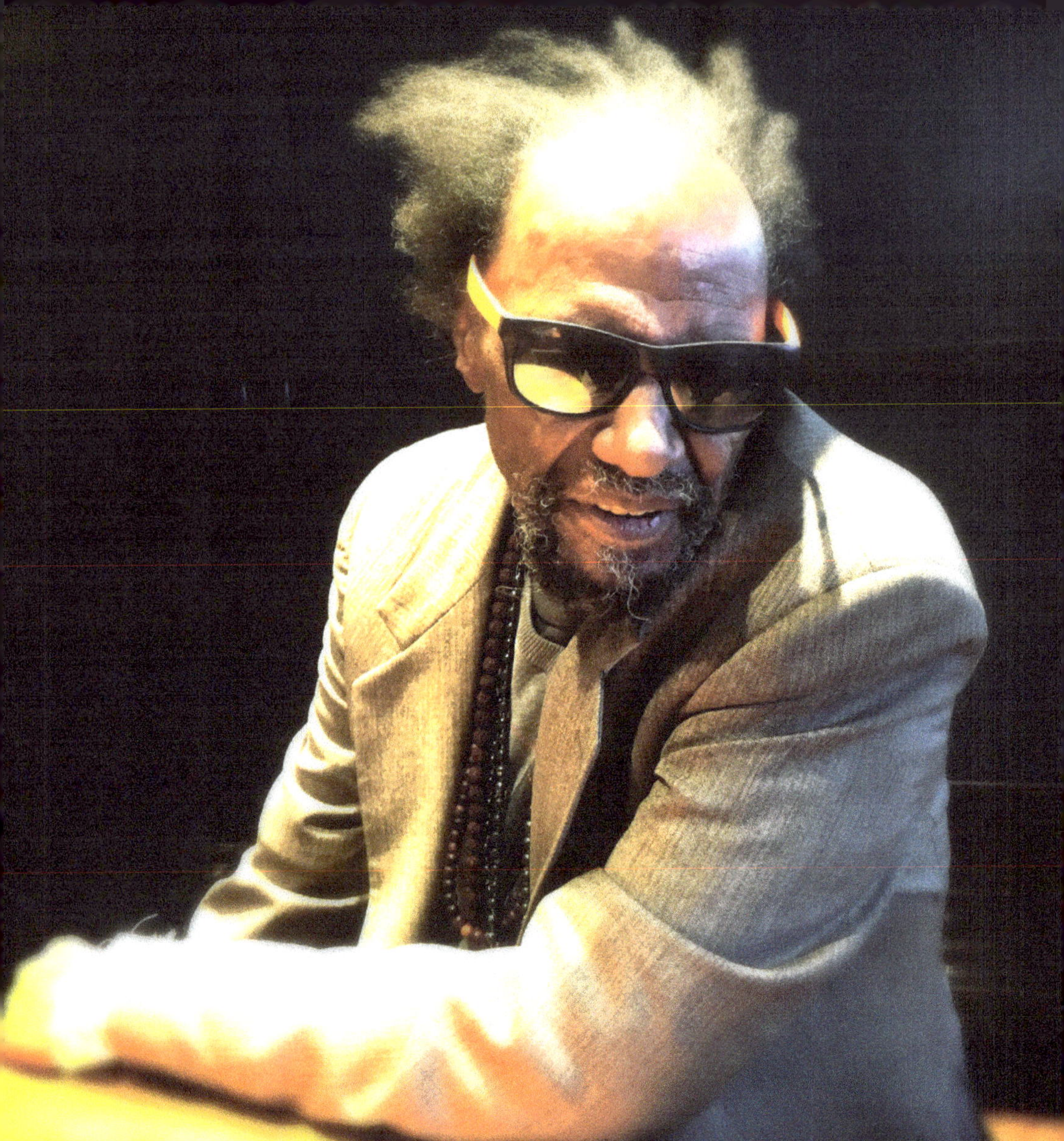

Foreword

I met Steve Cannon at his East Village home over 25 years ago. For those of you who haven't had the great pleasure of knowing Steve Cannon, he is the blind publisher, mentor, and patriarch that the *New York Times* says, "has helped foster roughly 50 years of New York's avant-garde history — often from his couch." When I met Steve, I had just lost my father in New Orleans and was up to any adventure that could suffocate my grief. Steve's living room was filled with painters, poets, bohemians, red wine, and a sculpture made of afro hairballs left behind in Harlem barber shops strung together like planets in the solar system. This art piece hovered over the usual magnetic mayhem of Steve Cannon's home and gallery on East 3rd St.

He was the archetypal guru of his smoky parlor, sitting between young, giggling women whispering in his ear, dangling their legs over his lap. Everyone in the room was vying for Steve's attention— they wanted to read their poems aloud and hear the honest critiques of the wise, blind poetry professor which sometimes sounded like, "boo, boo, boo, or yawn, yawn, yawn."

Poet and Slam Master Keith Roach brought me to Steve's after a night at the Nuyorican Poets Cafe. "Steve, I brought your homegirl from New Orleans here."

"What he said? Somebody from New Orleans...?"

The room shushed. Steve singled me out — laughing with a familiarity that brought me back to the men that were my dad's friends in New Orleans. The convo about our hometown oozed with New Orleans laid-down vowels and the ends of words not important enough to pronounce. I was happy to know New Orleans was giving me an important new friend and mentor, and after leaving home to explore New York, this fathering and familiarity was just what I needed. I read a poem to Steve that night, and was suddenly born to a movement of writers, poets, actors, artists, and friends that have continued to entertain me, love me, hold space for me, and make art with me.

It took 25 years of New York City love, living, readings, struggle, play-making, dues-paying, loneliness, and healing to get this particular book out. I am entirely grateful that Steve Cannon is publishing this work after waiting so long for me to "get it together."

These poems were saviors to the latest transitions in my life. There are many ghosts in this book — ghosts of friends who passed away and ghosts of friendships that were severed. There's my fascination with body and food, blood, familial roots and the eclectic nature of my own spiritualism mixed with Catholicism, dreams, saints, haints, haunts, the ancestors, and other dimensions. There's also good friends, meanness, cats and catty-ness, single life, married life, and many iterations of the woman surviving in between.

Black Jelly also features the raw, real, fresh, sexy, irreverent and intimate photos of my very dear friend, Nikki Johnson, whom I have found to be one of the most intriguing women and artists of our time. I am thankful for the honesty that is exhibited in any one of Nikki Johnson's photos, and I am glad that *Black Jelly* features not only her objective work, but the personal photos Nikki has taken during our friendship over the years.

Of course, it was Steve Cannon that introduced me to the maverick orb that is Nikki Johnson. At the time, we were both young artists far-flung from our southern homes, living in the East Village. But now — we "grown," living in Harlem, bringing you this *Black Jelly*. Welcome to the adventure of our tremendous sorrows, the beauty of finding home wherever you stand, the chicken skin, the back of a man's neck, the bones, the bulge, the empty beds, and God. We hope you see yourself in any of these bellies, these bras, this beauty, this celebration of eccentricity, and the formlessness of being a woman, while stomping grief to death.

JUMPING

OFF THE PORCH

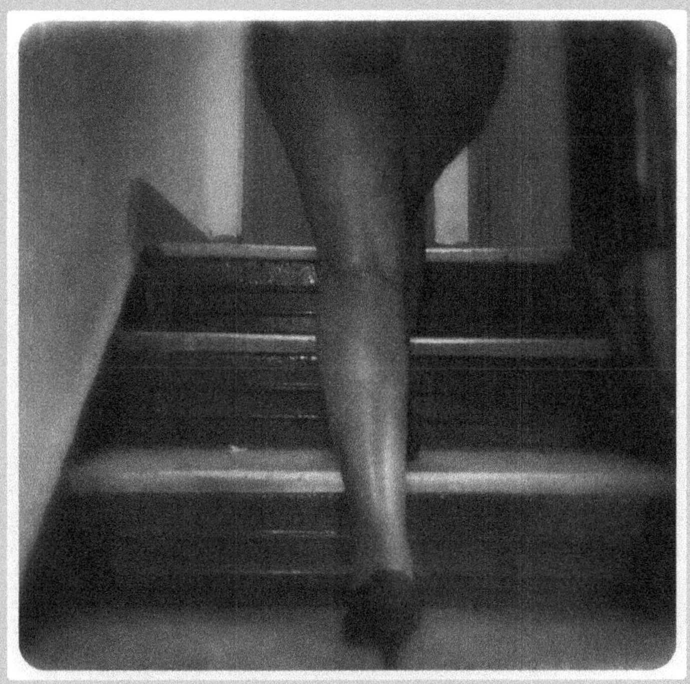

Free Falling Fallopian

I. FALLOPIAN

She decided
>> to throw

>> her Fallopian tubes
>> into the waste paper basket

>> along with her theological essay

o
n

c
o
m
p
a
r
i
n
g

>> Mary and Martha from the book of Luke

Success and failure

b r o k e

into pieces of

m e m o r y.

II. THIGHS

She couldn't

                              pick up
                              anything

from the foundation

of loose floor planks
and haphazard nails

                              dark blood

                              messed up
                              notebook pages
                              of hope and nonsense

menses
dried
into crust

she cut away the past from her thighs

                              and researched body lifts
                              and armo-plasty on the internet

she google-searched
she washed the dishes.

Two Cents Offering

wop wack
boogie black
bump blank
lonely lady
bossy bug

manless bitch
awkward naked
coat-covered kitten
fat face
supple sin

Jesus jumping
tambourines, opinions
nobody wants
your damn
opinion all
the time

stomach aches
sugar binging
pipe smoking
clouds of
where am
I, huh?

fat feast
swollen beast
monster-greed
Popeyes fried
chicken thighs

heavy load
switch code
tight clothes
piss quick
urine stream
lettuce, please

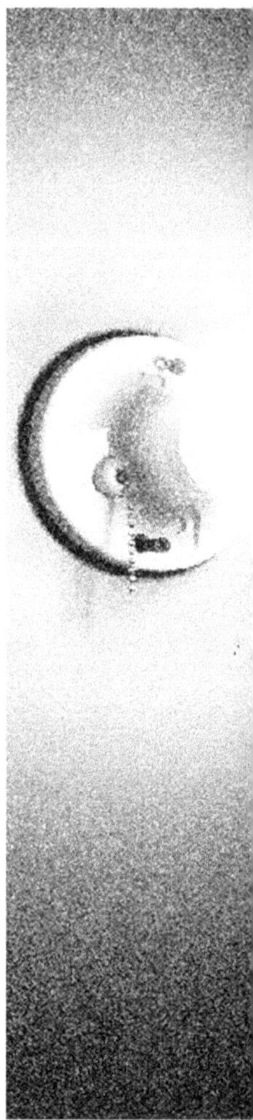

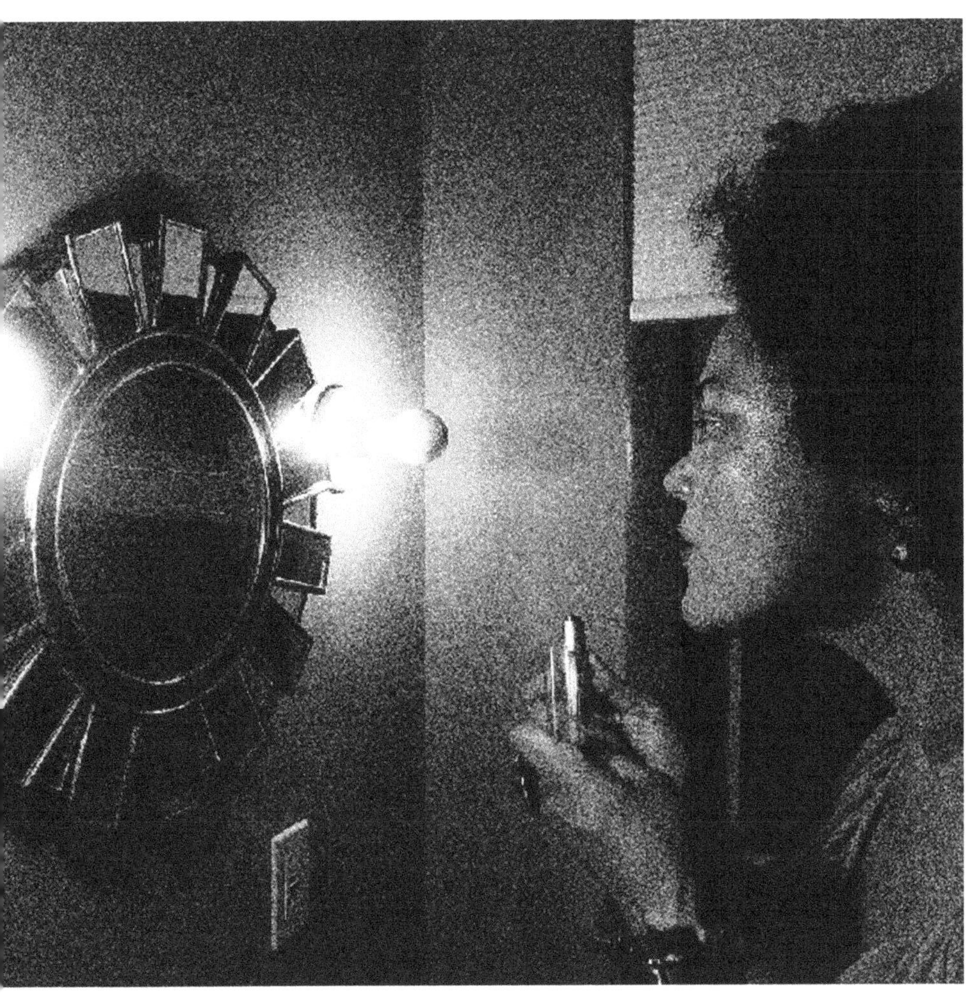

thin excuses
cheeky comfort
lazy daughter
of God
Stop telling
me what
to do.

Incarnation of Buttery Bread

I. BLACKTOP BLOOD

One girl jumping between

karma   and   incarnations

skipping rope with the

l
o
n
g
e
s
t

of legs.

When she falls down

good blood runs out of her knees

and
lands
on
asphalt.

She butters bread with this memory.

II. WIGGLE

One girl jumping between

karma   and   hot pink teenage walls
                                          of property purchased
                                          by a black man in the 1960s

skipping rope

                   with the
                                          t
                                          h
                                          i
                                          c
                                          k
                                          e
                                          s
                                          t

                                          of big ol' legs.

When she falls down
                                          the dimples on her thighs wag/wiggle

                                                        and
                                                        land
                                                        on
                                                        black jelly.

She butters bread with this memory.

III. BED OF BIG BODIES

One girl jumping between

karma   and   the ceiling of a Harlem loft bed

a nest
of mismatched covers
for lovers

entangled
big bodies of sex and love

skipping rope with the

f
a
t
t
e
s
t

of fat- fine legs

sweet enough to bite.

When she falls down   good spirit leaps out of her chest
and lands
on chalk marks for hopscotch.

She butters bread with this memory.

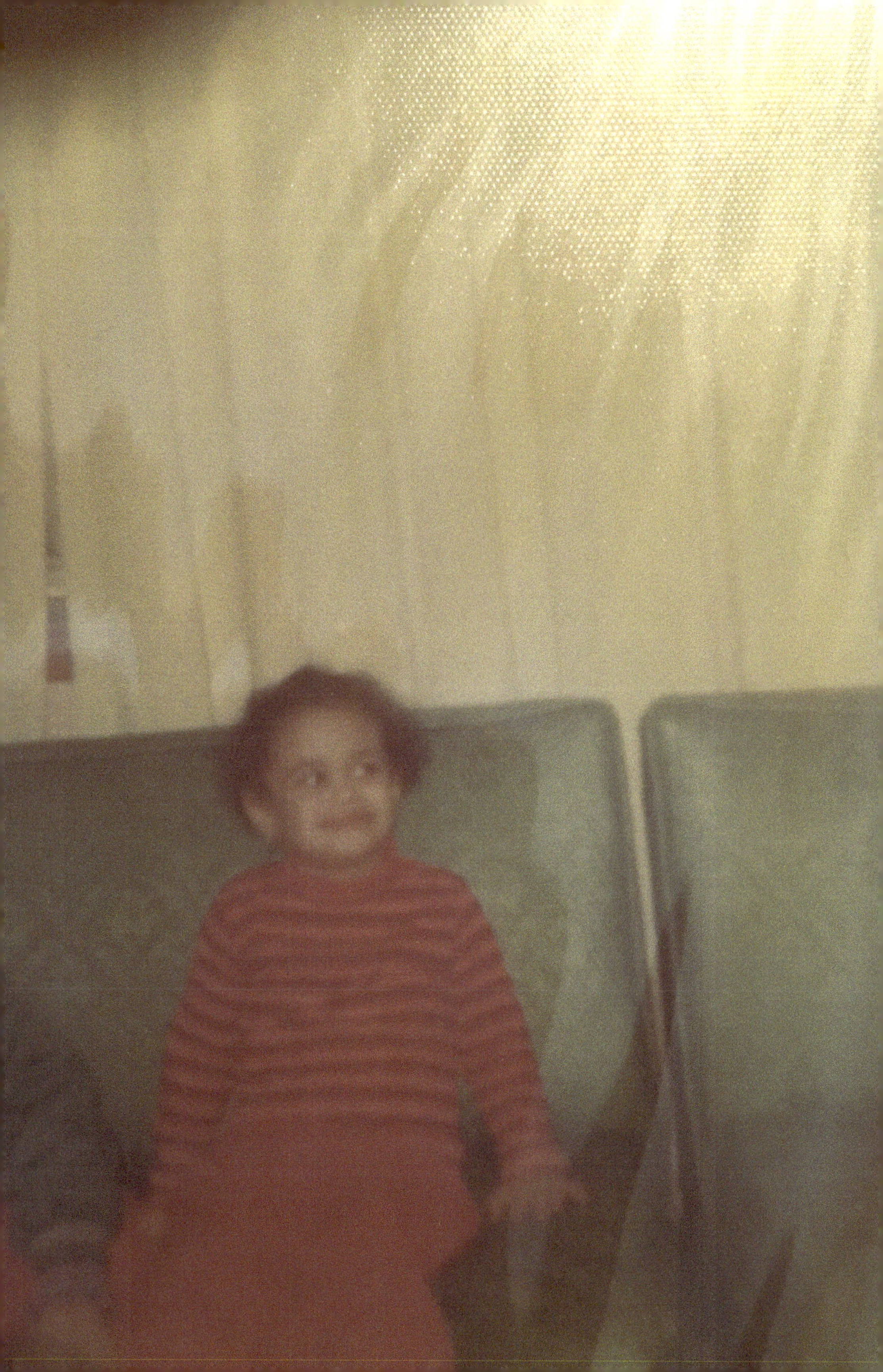

Hymns of Haphazard Home

I. EAST VILLAGE LAMENT

And the blind man was at home

> in the grey darkness

> since his sight
> and all light
> had been yanked away

and the off-mother was at home
> in her grief

> since her three children
> had been kidnapped

and her ass was at home
> in the aqua-blue silk sundress

> that had a hole
> in the underarm

and the Puerto Rican boys were at home

> in the dump of bricks

> caved in from hollowed out
> tenements

swinging there on ropes tied to beams

> at home in the hope
> that they may or may not
kill themselves

their laughter
bouncing off bricks
and swollen emptiness

> in echoes

their hunger
at home in their bellies

healed by
swiping benefits cards

urban Tarzans defying gravity.

II. HYMN OF BRA AND PANTYHOSE

The tooth in my mouth
was at home

until she yanked it out.

The blood in my toe
was at home

until she drove a nail inside of it
with a power drill.

Home
was

tight
pantyhose
rubbing together

between
tight thighs
in tight
moments.

Home
was
the nagging bra

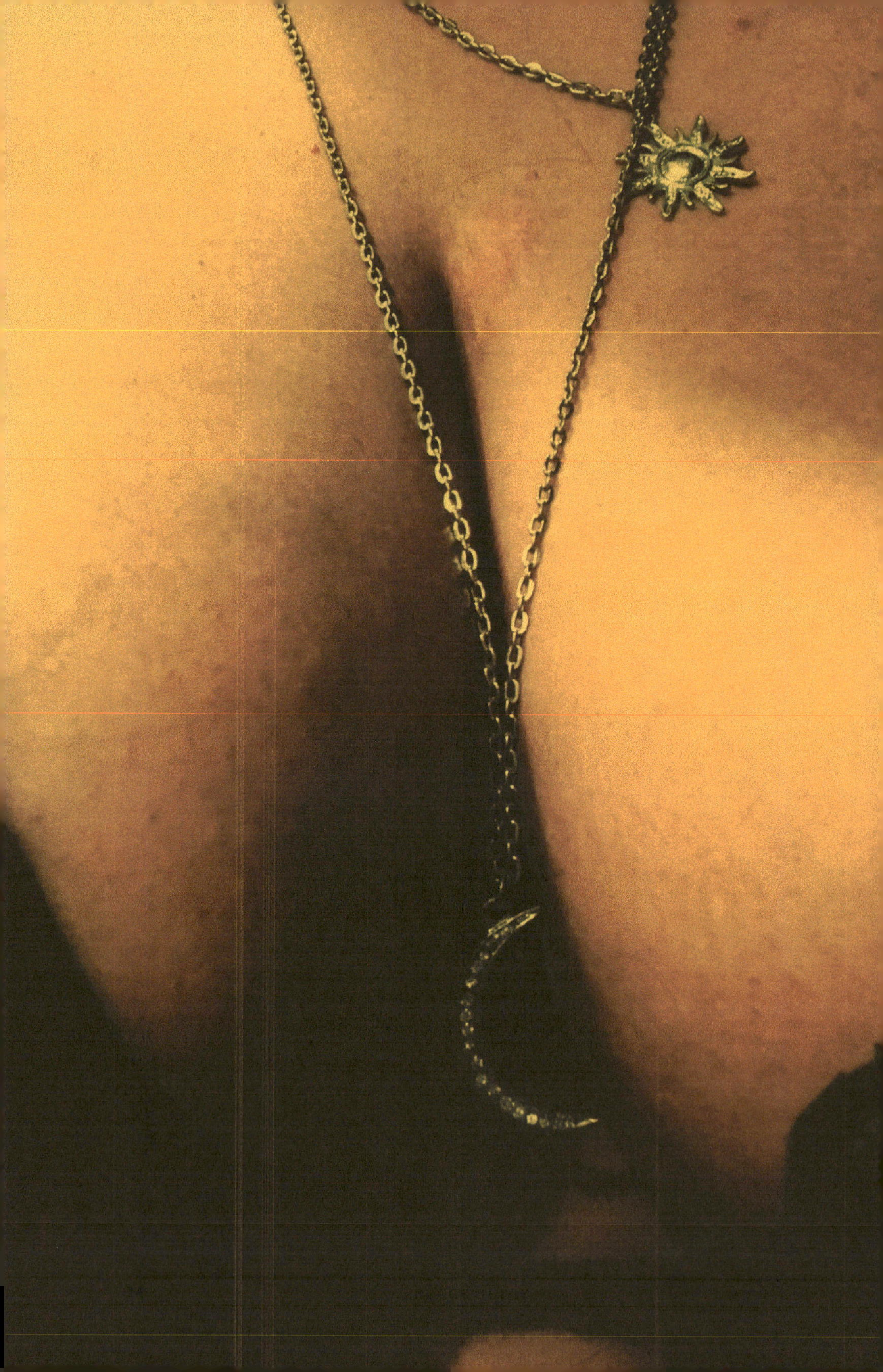

gnawing its teeth
into my fat folds of skin

                        cutting off my circulation

                        the nagging bra
                        fastened at the farthest clasp
                        a hook gone

a connection crooked

                        twisted into uselessness

my fat tits

            falling out
            of
            home

                        with the bra

                        bra
                        mad at the rolls

                        bra
                        mad at the rolls of fat

            blood bulging
            beneath wires

            and too tight ties

                        knots
                        nights
                        nipples

            discomfort.

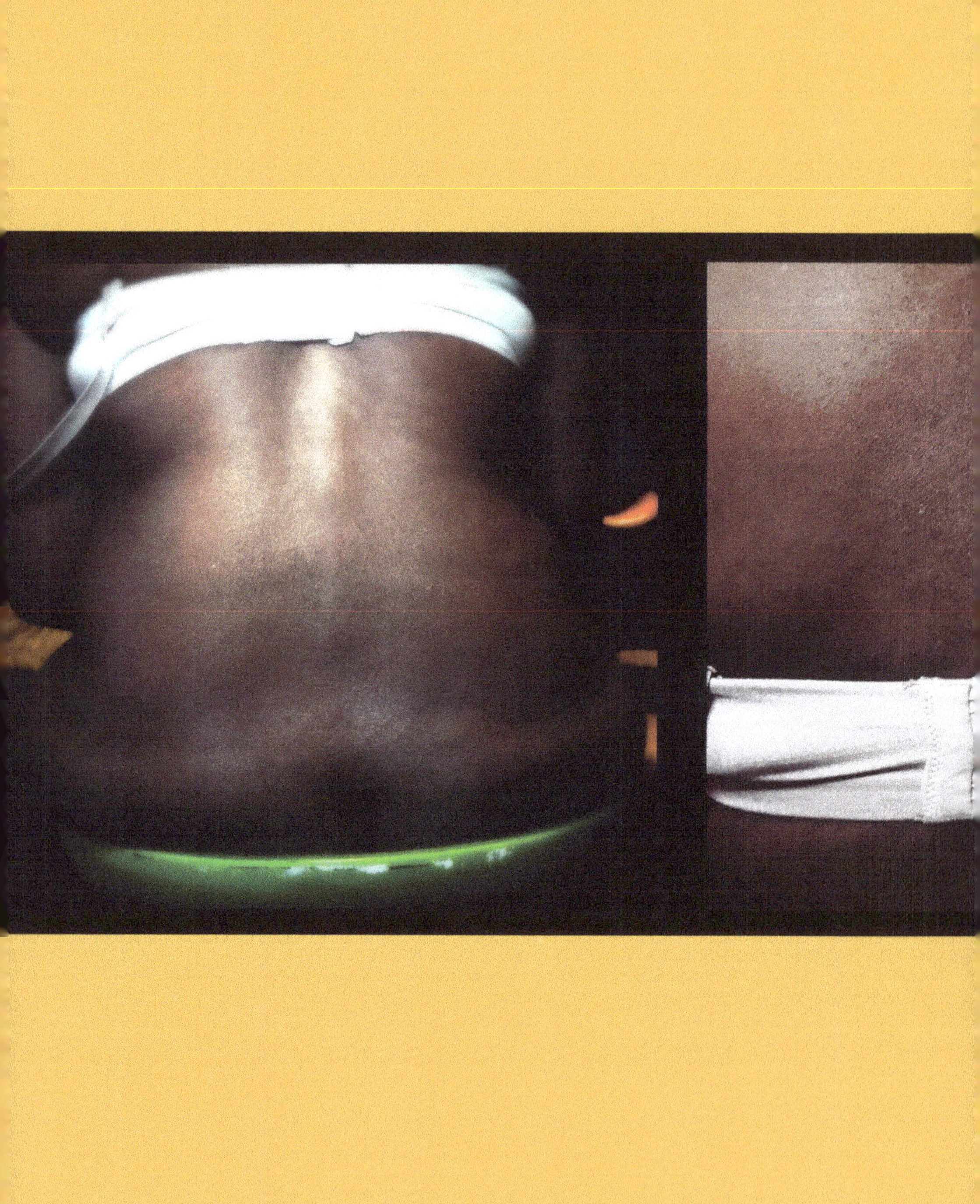

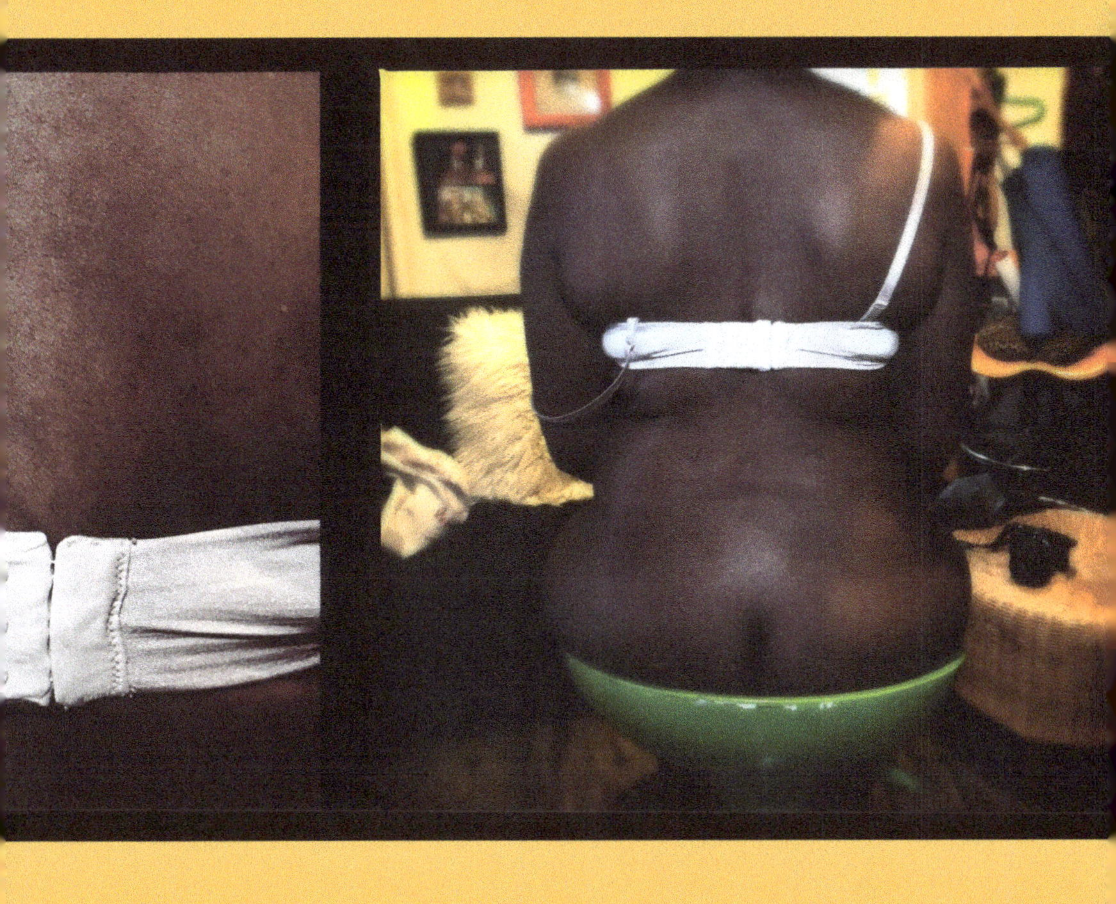

III. CRUMBS AS FLAMBEAUX FOR PRODIGAL WOMAN

Did you leave anything behind for the fat woman coming down the road?

Skeletons tap-dance on graves
witches trapped in ovens
flambeaux carriers twirl and jook

not   enough   air   to   blow   a   trumpet   well

bones baking
spirits taking
account   of who lived there before

at home   in the grief of generational beef

crumbs of bones   good and bad blood

each crumb
the last bit of food
meant for   black bird
                                      snake
                                      goat
                                      or
                                      desperate prodigal woman

                                      to swallow

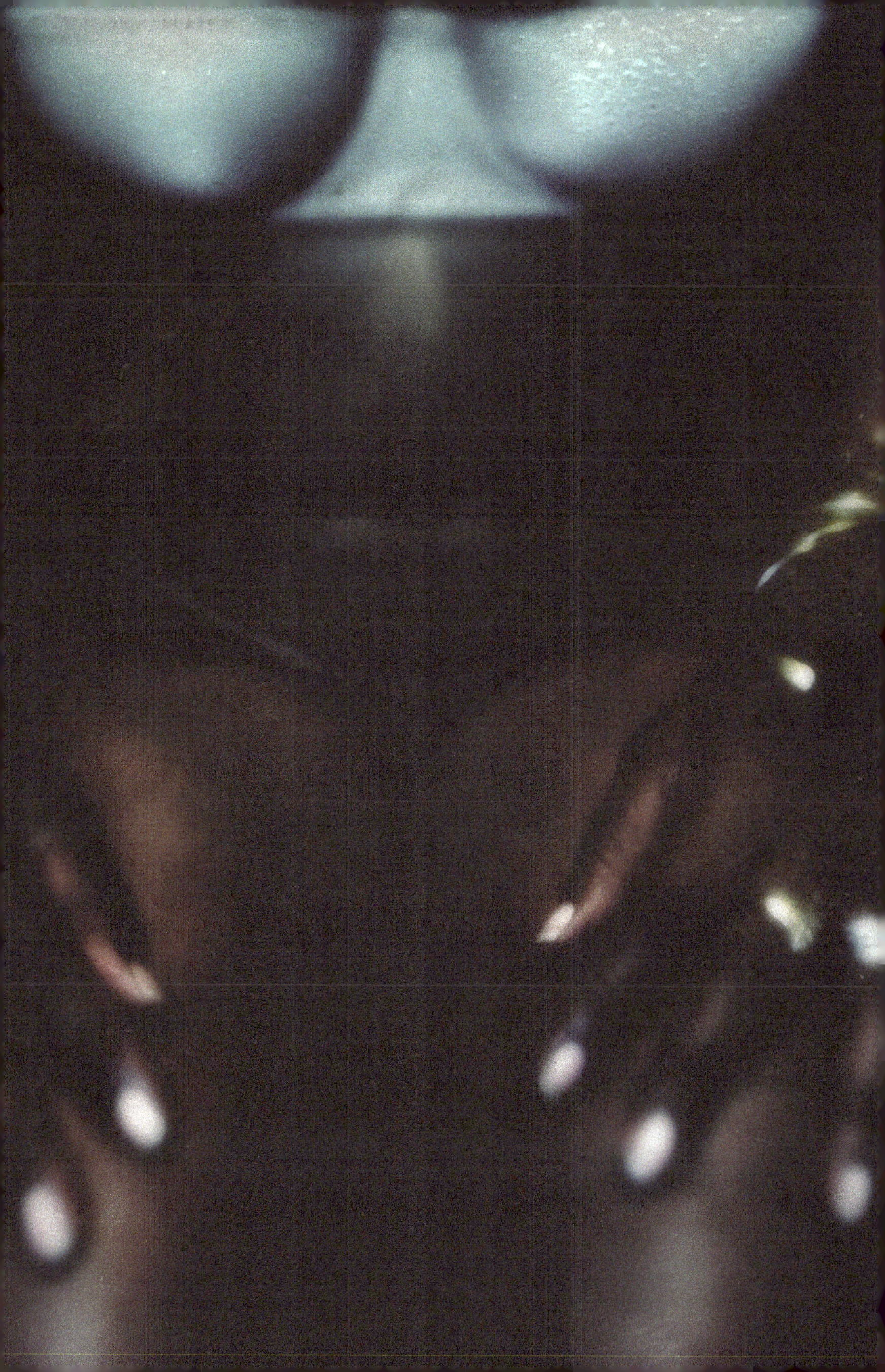

IV. HYMN OF PORK CHOP

Pork chops live in grease
and lay on top of paper towels
on the stove

it's okay to eat two

at home
with the white Wonder Bread
from the fridge.

V. BLUE VINES

Blue vines
big white thighs

purple confusion
of varicose

teeth
                work
                            hours
                                    food

there's nothing in the refrigerator
to connect with for later.

VI. LUCKY CRUMBS

Home

crumb of memory

                    left behind on the Teflon

                    each crumb

                    some home

                    lucky
                    to fall out of my mouth.

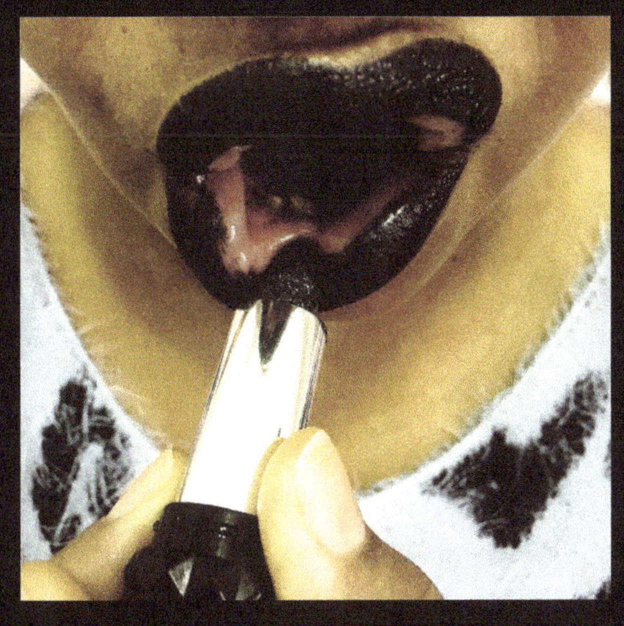

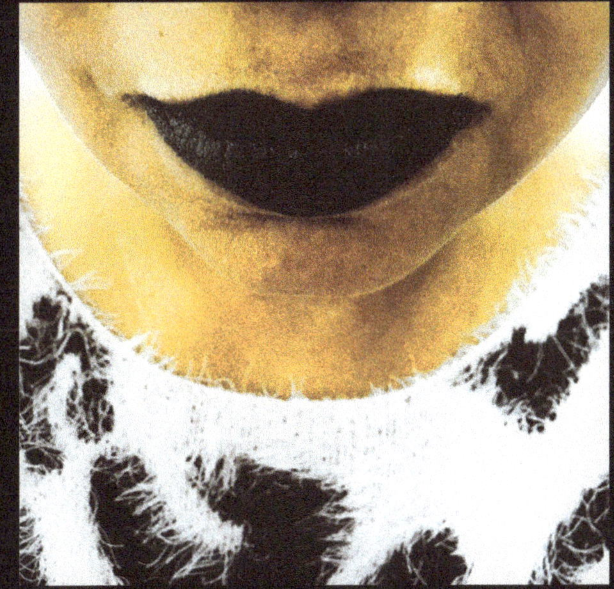

Thirsty Cold Lady

So cold that day in the East Village

my wine glass   of water
turned to ice   filled solid to the brim
a figurine

                                   frozen
                                   in
                                   time.

It looked like   a white
                   and icy flamingo
                   emerging

                   from
                   frigid floorboards

                   balancing on
                   one
                   cold
                   leg

                   emptied
                   of its hot pink color

an ice sculpture sitting by the toilet

                   ice-glazed glass and thirst
                   emerging from the wood
                   ready to burn my fingers

I trip on the nail I hammered into the floor
                   reaching
                   for the splash of ocean

                   once meant to be gulped for revival
                   now held still

by your frosty sorcery

a manipulated cold   you created

by flipping switches.

My breath was a visible cloud of cold,
January in New York
the chilling apartment you broke into   was hard to heat

with one jittery space heater
going hot-orange
in thin lines
of electric fire   *the bill was paid*
                                                              I had paid the bill

                                                              the bill was paid
                                                              I had paid the bill

but not the 500 dollar punk dues for being stupid.

My bosom can't make ribbons out of facts:

you singled out the breaker
to my apartment
                              turning off my electricity
                              taking time with tools
                              in the middle of a January blizzard
to keep me shivering —
                              me
                              black woman,
                              daughter of someone good,
                              at your service for so long.

How many garbage cans filled with the bottom-of-NYC-randomness
did I turn over
                              avoiding every rat I could?

Sitting on the toilet
frozen into a block
                              the hiss of piss left me

ice-skidding urine
the only friend of mine.

Pretending

You have to pretend that the house is empty
and that the only thing you're coming home to is the curtains
even if you don't have curtains.
Pretending is not so bad —
it's a course taught in college that you can take.

No one is there.

You can not become attached to any particular sentences.
None of the words there really belong to you.
Even your own words back are a teleplay script.
This is all okay. Never sour. Drink protein shakes.

Do not take any fat fighting pills.

Concentrate on the images you really want to visit with.
You are only offering so much of yourself
'cause you think people are there.

It's only you.

Everyone else is a piece of art. Pretend with a smile.
Know your own happy secrets. Make some up.
You are five years old at home in your mother's blue nightgown.
Pretending is easy for you.

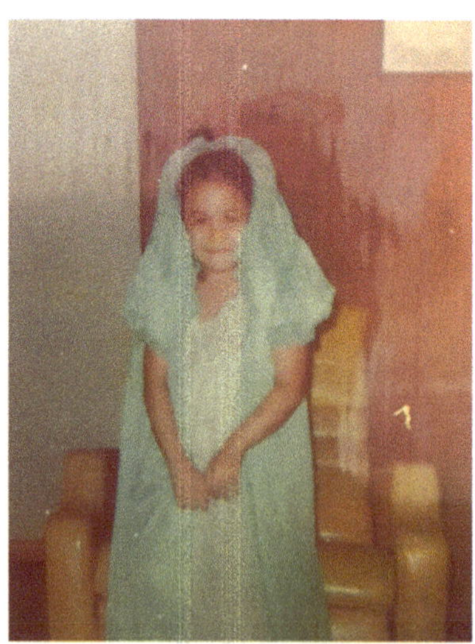

Belonging

You are not an orphan.
You belong to the chipping paint on the purple house
the   black   painted   night

                                                the blackened gum globs
                                                on the ground
                                                that spell out your name

you belong to Portuguese lyrics
you heard on a record
revolving for the room in circles and sound

                                                coming back to you
                                                from an ancestor

you belong to the pain
that ceases to be after:

two minutes   two hours   two days   two weeks
two months   two years   two decades two lifetimes

you belong to   the songs you never sang because you were so busy

you belong to   the tender space of being spanked by God,
                so get up!

                the cold wind of apprehension stops you at each door,
                but go in!

You belong to   the wing   the beak   the chicken
                the yard   the plate   you eat from.

You don't want to see

                those scrapes   the cuts   the marks
                those cold fingers   the skiffs   the bones

the swollen-bellied   dogs   howling.

You don't want to see a rising pool of Mississippi River

                              coming up to drown
                              your house in brown

and leave its mildew mark along your walls

                              the mud-faced dolls
                              of plastic white baby girls tossed
                              into distortion and disheveled nakedness

blonde hair in a ditch
that won't keep well through trouble and pretending

She didn't belong to you
                              in the first place
neither the broken dishes
or the faces you once knew with birthday cake

the ones you won't ever see again

                              nor the silence
                              that divides you
                              for more than many miles.

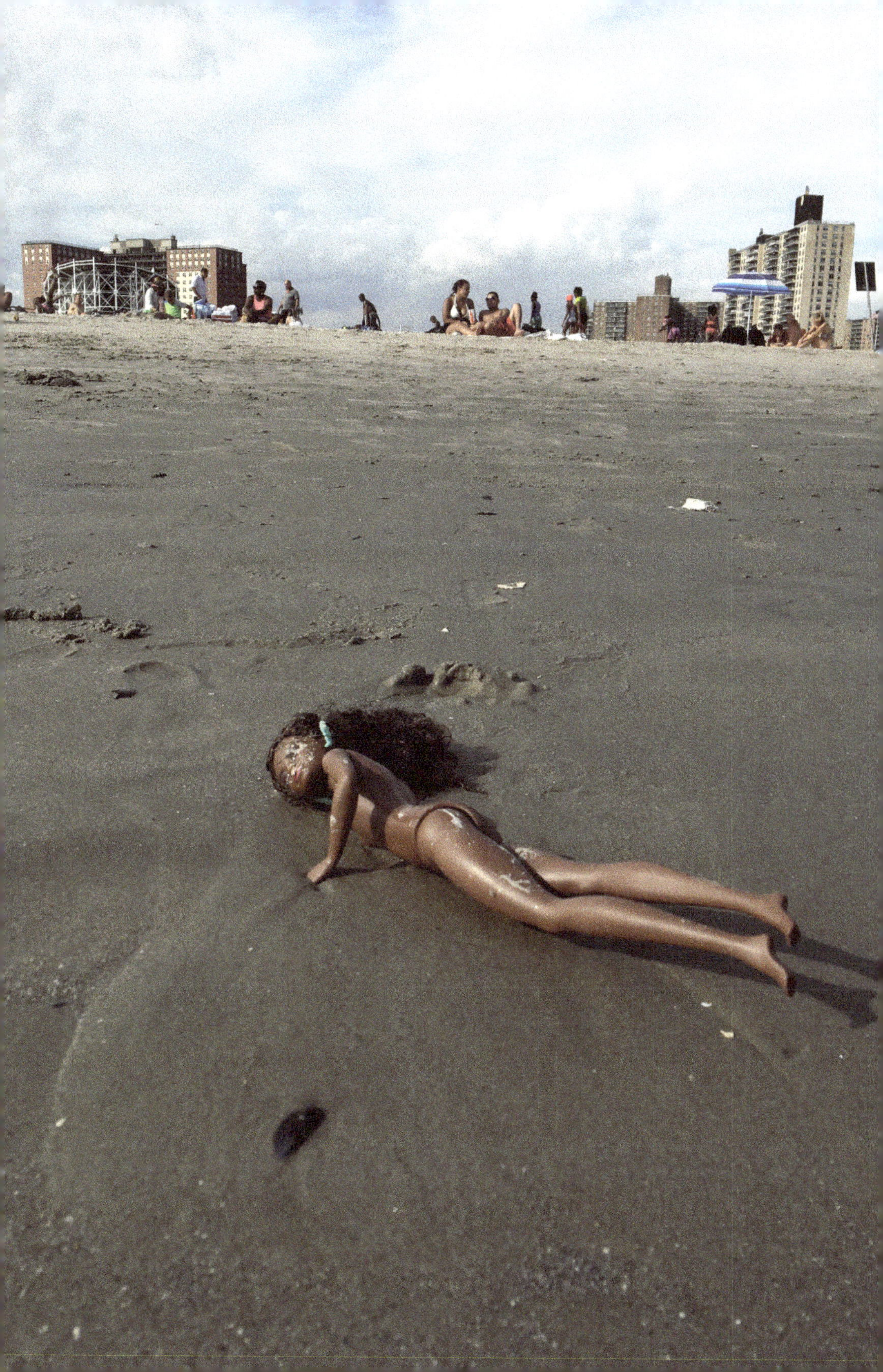

Queen of Swerve

All I have

is this foot —
                                    this foot
            his foot
            his big toe
                  hard/ dry
                                the one given to my lap

                                something to caress
                                something to squeeze blood from
                                something to believe in

All I have

is this Butterfinger
                                something to get me home
                                something to take away
                                the knot of thoughts

an orange crunch of sugar

a cheap chocolate saint to be

                                toppled with my tongue
                                melting in my mouth
                                swallowing a mounting sorrow
a cheap chocolate saint to be
                                devoted to

All I have

are these letters
                                stained with coffee and age
                                lucky to find each page
                                in a yellowing envelope of passing time
                                the ones my father left behind

                              I was a sweet girl he cherished
                              on motel stationery
                              in words
                              and cartoon bubbles

                              restoring my faith in destiny
                              after his own heart
                              stranded him out there

                              with nothing beating inside

                              the ambulance 30 minutes late
                              so he died.

All I have
                              are these mustard seeds of God
                              so small
                              you might miss them
            even worse you might diss them

oh, the pillows I keep fluffing
for the egos I keep stuffing

            how many sidewalks I turned with faith
            the places I've been where I shouldn't have been
            the night I hung with a gangsta with gold-teeth and gun
            the night the A train conductor let me steer
            the subway down its tunnel for fun
            the time each sham-holy-man wanted love from me
            the night some bitch fed a gaggle of mice in my bedroom
            with my Chinese food on Avenue D
            squeaking feeding frenzy in grey
            crawling over my floor
                                    or the day

            I got a credit card that took me to Spain
                                    on an airplane

thinking the machine was its own God of get me from here to there
flying in the air
                  without a care

All I have

      is this credit card
      this little blue rectangle of money
      that is never really mine

All I have   is this faith

      the night Mo Batz saved me in a yellow cab at 4 a.m.
      I was running away from some cray-zah man

all I had   was my pretty
all I had   was my naivety
all I had   was my red lipstick
all I had   was a dollar twenty-five to keep me alive

All I have   is this hair
                the hair I shaved off

                buzzing my cut
                acting like a slut
                      so what

                the hair I set on fire
                singing hail marys
                in the kitchen

                the hair someone grabs for dear life

                the hair someone styles
                in my heaven on earth
                moments as a wife

                the hair that falls out
                in the shower
                with power

                the hair I know with full faith
                has dandruff

Forgive me for my honesty
                        and the smell
                        passing through the air
turning around your chair

all I have   is this fart

                            the one I just passed for gas

                            the thing I can pull from my ass

                            to save my life in a minute

all I have   is this crude
all I have   is this begging
all I have
                            is this reasoning
                            that I wish you could adopt in peace
all I have
                            is what I turn around and around all day
                            thinking of a better way

my body is warm

filled with the confusing messages
of Temple vs McDouble with Mac sauce

my body is safe

filled with Confucian messages of pain versus chakras spinning right

my body is a playground of faith

            with twisted messages of tingling toes
                                and manipulatable big breasts

My body: first comes health,
            then comes peace of mind,
            then comes wealth,
            then what you left behind:

My body: tarnished blessing of flesh for someone else
                        to pick up and draw upon
                        faith running up the treadmill

legs   move through mud
mind   writes through crud
lungs   open and swallow and breathe
allergies   make me sneeze
my body   is a test:

                        one titty

goes east   the other prefers west

All I have   is this foot
                                                and that one there

                        bruised ankles
                        weight to bear

blood   collected nerves

big tits   and curves

This   is   how   I   swerve.

                    BLACK JELLY

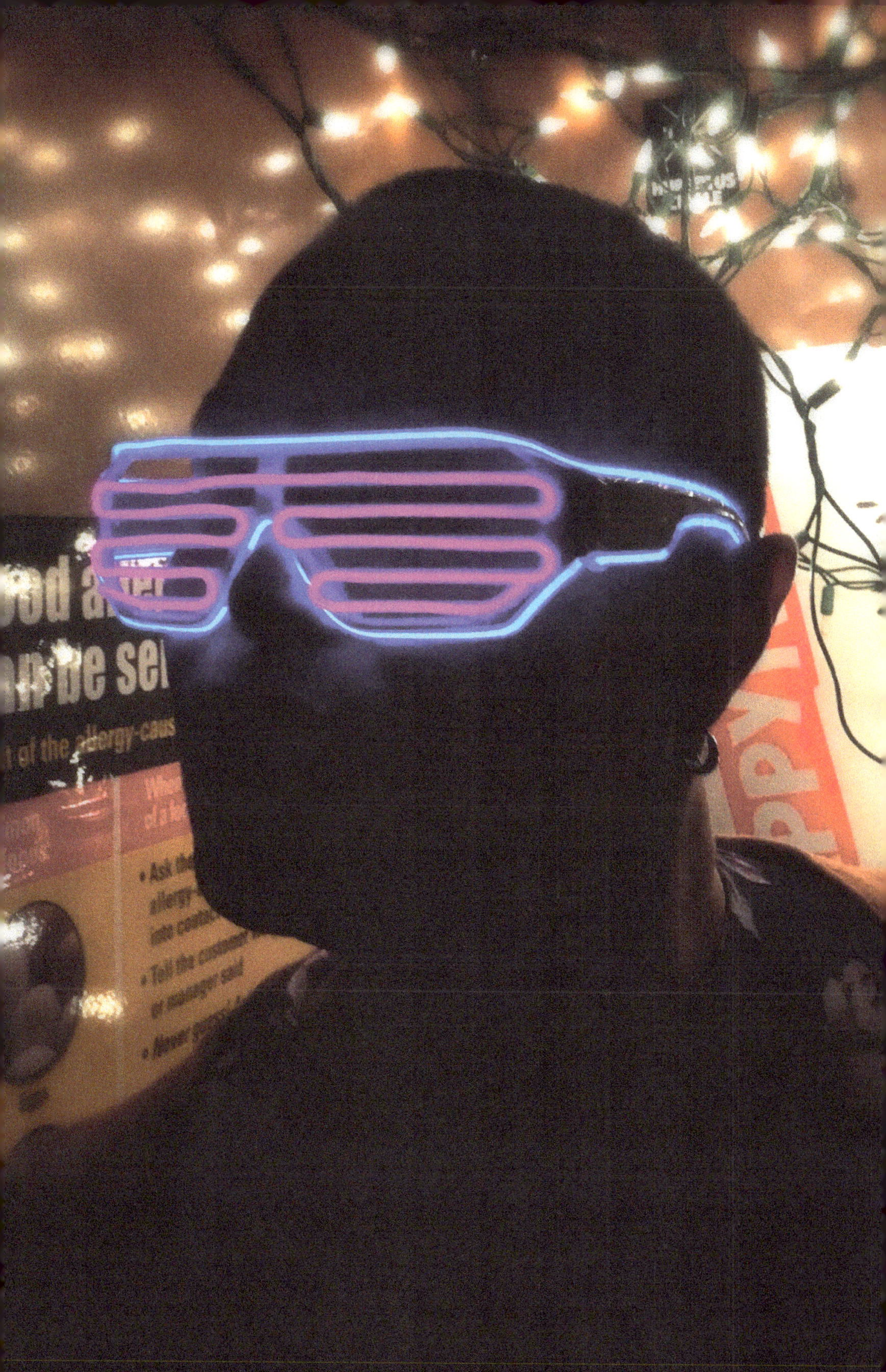
od a
an be se
of the allergy-cau
HAPPY

SPLIT

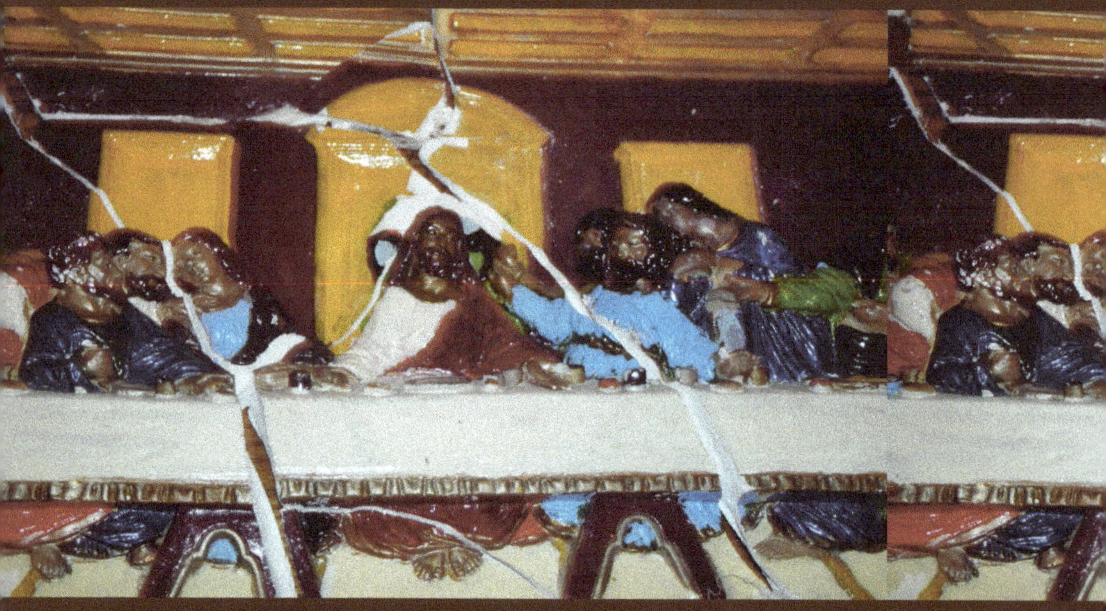

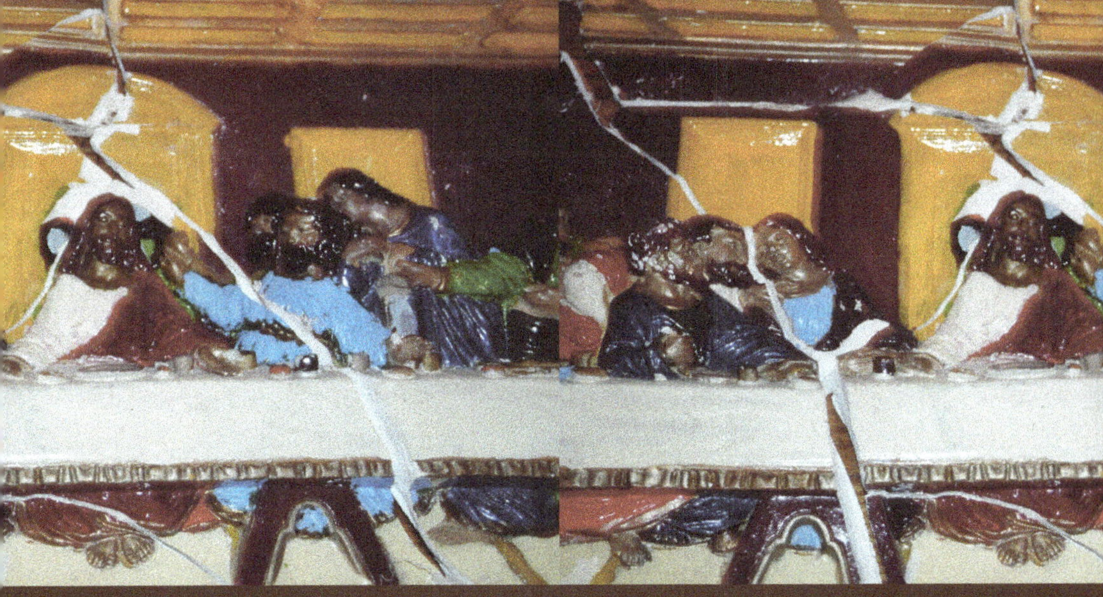

2

ENDS

Witch to Me

I. SPOTTING THE THOUGHT OF CLARA

And just at that moment

I thought I saw Clara
pointing to the poem of the moment
free of the seaweed
normally stuck in her teeth

pointing to the poem that had outlived her.

Clara was an astrologer and a poet
a conversationalist on a raw food diet

many times she chewed on spinach leaves
and talked with a mouth full of dark green munch

a white girl
who I both loved and was annoyed by

she ran a race with cancer on her own
without crying every time I ran into her on the train
a mantra entered my brain
informed by Clara's memory and active appearance

Witch to me
is experiencing a little bit of Heaven on the Earthly dimension —

like a ghost:

don't die on the vine at this time or next time
don't die on the vine at this time or next time
don't die on the vine at this time or next time
don't Die
on
the
Vine

II. JABEZ A-LOOSE

And then, I checked my phone
for a message I knew wasn't there

and remembered how I had also lost Jabez as a friend

that he was a-loose
                              somewhere

roaming
                      in a
                                      wander

a path down farther
                                      yonder

a   w   a   y   from me

not due to Heaven or Hell or drowning:

His departure so hard to swallow
the bitch-assed-ness where I wallow

Me?

Grieving the dead
Grieving the living
Grieving

a match set to ease
burning   us
                                      down to the ground

emblazoned back shed of dry wood
taking to spontaneous combustion caused by
the beta alpha female chicken
scratching heat into the junky twigs of his chicken coop

twigs and fags
twigs and fags
twigs and fags
                                      chicken scratch and frogs
                                      chicken fat and hogs

III. GERTRUDE STEIN IN A BOX

And then I remembered   Gertrude Stein
how I saw her in a play last night in

                                    a black box
                                    a black box
                                    a black box

a play
a play

on wanting
a new friend that was also an envelope to open
a new friend that was a kind letter to read
a new friend that was a blue bowl worthy enough to sell or keep forever

not like a text
that would roam like a specter
through the grey wet wool of cut-out love
kindness brought to a halt by insecurity
and a very bad opera song that I was sweet enough to applaud for

                                    his voice wilting way down
                                    terribly and loudly

                                    into a hollow memory

                                    I'd like to forget

IV. PARIAH-PLAYAH

I left this poem and others too.

        Tell them, Clara
        say something weird
        from gone dimension.
I keep abandoning it

to go to class
to eat too much
to take photos of my tax forms
to lay in a way inviting to the fat black rump of my cat on the bed
to lay

I keep leaving

the words escaping my spirit
like feet pedaling miles on a rusted bike quickly

        moving ahead

I may try to save them

        less fragile than friendship
        less disposable leper
        less disposable pariah

though my husband calls me   play-ah

        playah   pariah
        playah   pariah
        playah   pariah
the sighs
the woes to toes
poison of love

seeing these ghosts   and others

on the block   on the train
                of my brain.

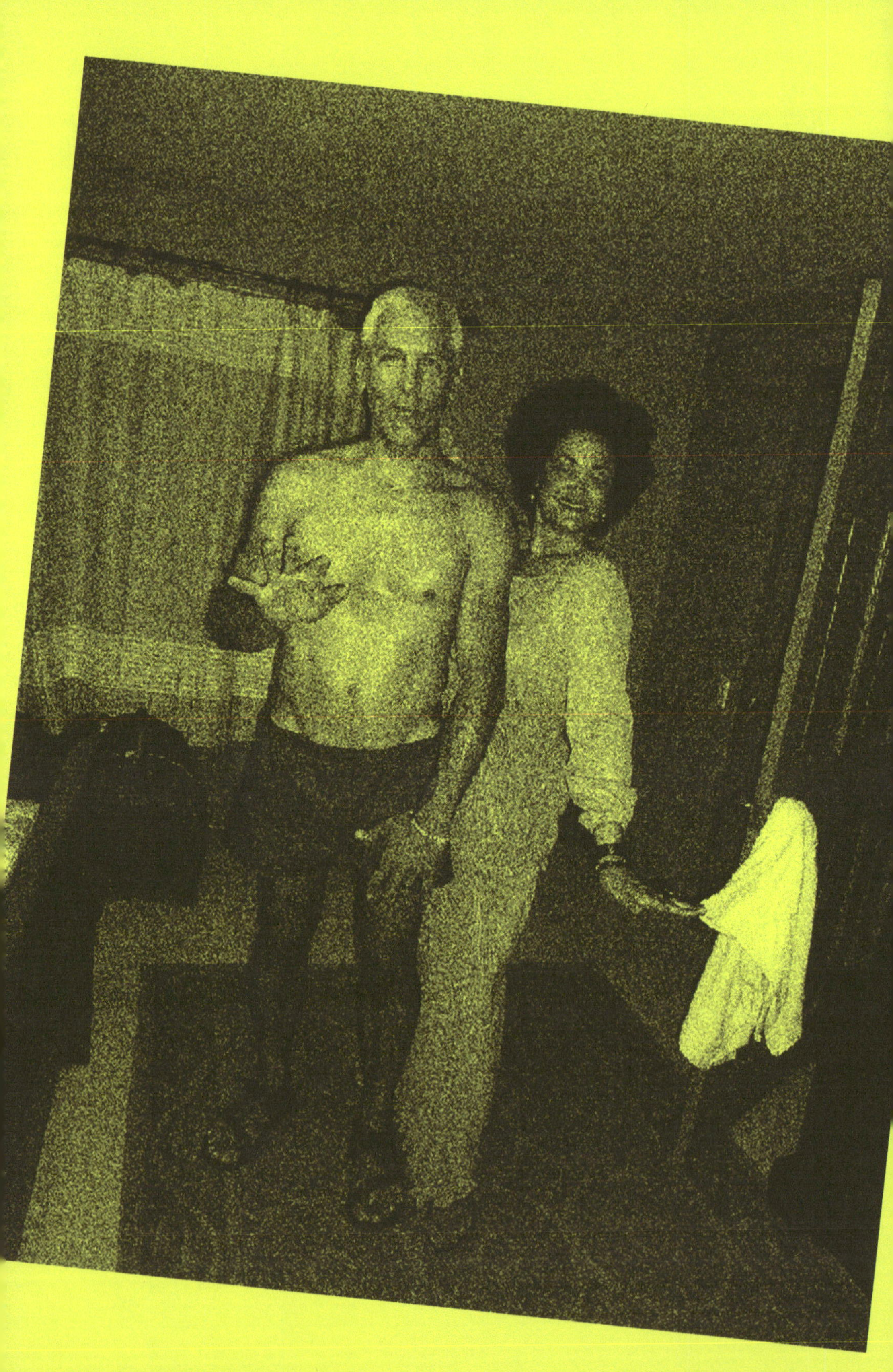

Thank You For Trying

I. ANGLES AND FORGIVENESS

My friend Matt
              is a walking amount of angles
                             and forgiveness

branches gathered up in his arms
raking Minky's yard
building a bar out of Mr. Sullivan's bed frames

He, himself   locomoting his character
                  across all the green of the lawn

He is a barnacle of bone

many shutters
of time
opening and shutting
        his eyelids
        one
        blink   at   a   time
mobs of shutters
a proletariat of portraits

working in the shed
mailing out the Mother's Day cards

There he is   my friend
always doing something
        putting a flame out with his donk
        rowing a boat for miles
        saying something stupid for smiles
        playing Ms. Pac-Man tilll we found loopholes in the game
        our eyes glossed over
        til Diane came home
        she and the American Spirits of life
        arriving to the basement floor apartment
        that Matt befitted with giant photos of sheep
        and giant photos of giant peeps to keep

II. CANDY-COLORED GHOSTS

Candy-colored ghosts we are-were
sitting on a red disco couch till it went south we are-were
Pac-Man eating in our ears

There he is
                              naked in the snow
                              naked in the lake
                                                        naked in the photo
                                                        naked in the ocean
                              naked in our religions
                              naked in our black jokes
                              our news commentary
                                                        naked in his costumes
                                                        naked in his trouble
naked in Diane's arms
naked
alone

crispy veggie bacon in the pan
a tuna melt man
styles for miles
                                        snacks
                                        tall and slick
                                        doing tricks with his clicks

wet pee photos of his dicks and his dicks and his dicks
                                          with his clicks
                                          and their tricks
burning a word deep inside his chest
for trying
the reversed swollen T-R-Y
never really surprised me, I don't know why
              T   R   Y
Did you try?   Did you cry?

a scar for near and far
read to himself in a hundred mirrors
see me
see me
see me
I see me
I see meeeeee

III. BARNACLE OF BONE

A barnacle of bone
dog of a bounty hunter
idol of art
                never idle

                        a barnacle of bone
                        dog of a bounty hunter
                        idol of art

                                            never idle

a barnacle of bone
a barnacle of bone
an idol of art
                never idle

drumsticks   kitties   drills   cameras   TV   cat domes
a   pulpit   in   the   yard

eyes that weep
eyes that weep
eyes that weep

master of light and flash
master of Vermont
going to take a picture in a dash
driving a car with his internal force
his feet sinking far deep into the ground
past the floor board
close to the engine's sound
motor man at the wheel
moving us around so we feel
his Flintstone feet and his soul moving fast as steel

this poem is way too predictable
for someone so unpredictable
and

the applications of all you know and learn and offer
in your Matt kindness and generosity
and
the comedy that slips
from your tight-ass muttering murmuring Matt lips
smart-assed philosophies

catty comical quips
lots of potato chips and dips

one time Matt was in a band that threw a potato at me
the loudness of your farts
the library you've made for us with and written by your own eyeballs.

IV. YOU ARE THE MOUNTAIN, THE DEW

You are the volcano
You are the margarita
You are the lake
the cabin
the convertible
the diet
the mountain
the dew
the campfire
the tent

Thorever and badass
Thorever hot, fine, and spanked
Thorever shared
Thorever lens
Thorever Bull/Boll love
Thank you for trying.

BLACK JELLY

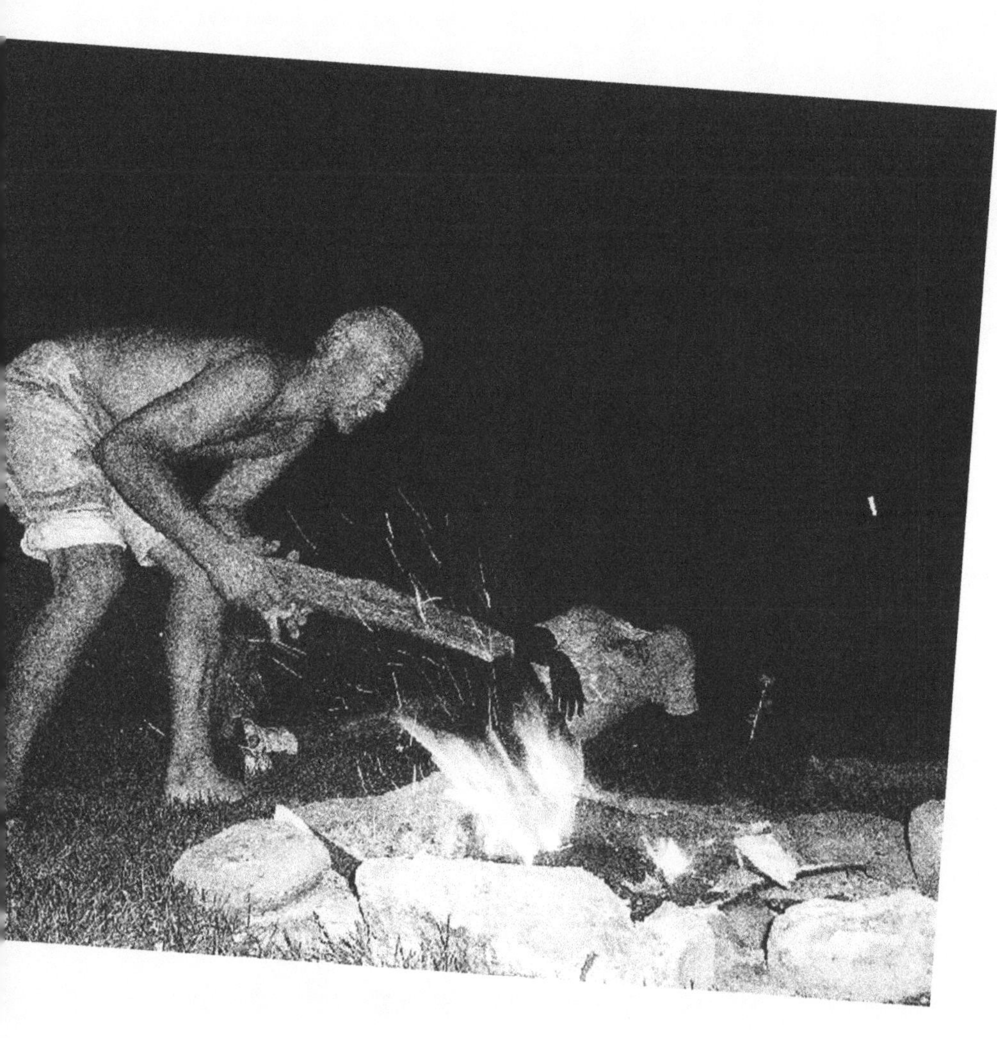

Escalator

She rolled her shoulders
each bony rotation
created smoke
a dry burn/fire of twigs

all the snakes inside of her churning
                twisting leathery turnings

no misgivings in her gnarled calculations
                sick like mossy trees

cursing the soft greying parted hair
                of her surroundings.

Why did I see her there?
Gliding down an escalator in the spiritual realm
                even before she left

                her shoulders
                the bones in her cheeks.

What —   has she come for me again?!

Where are her cats?   Are they starving?

Their stretching skeletons still haunting me
yowling around her bony high-yellow ankles.

Witch squabbling
over the heist of stolen blood she tried to hack out all at once
with a nail through my toe.

                Rim of flesh
                the scar

                a guiding star
                on my appendage.

Black Munstah

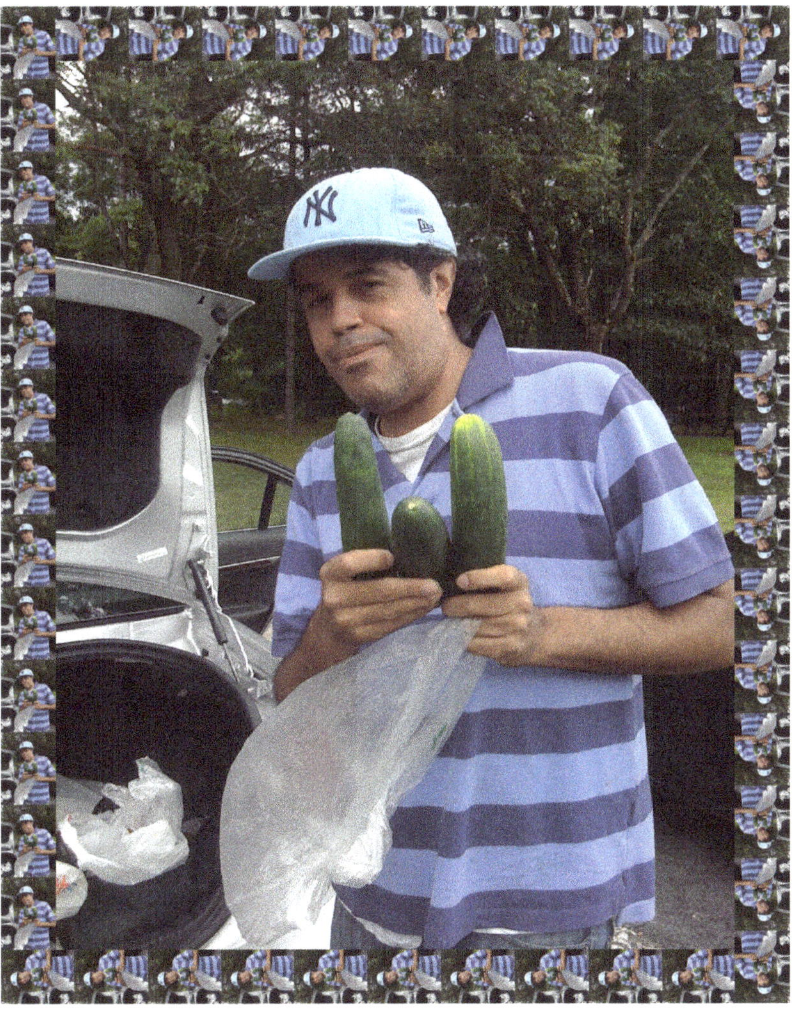

Munstah, dick-loving compadre,
shameless shade, ever-ready for Spades,
green cucumbers of love pointing towards your fetching grins.
A hat, a cap, a blue-*blue* cap,
a knitty, a cap, a blue-*blue* chap.

Where are your pickles?
Your Beanie Weenies?
Your complaints that rarely exist?
Your tight, awkward handshakes?

You were the truest of friends that ever-endured
fights, briskets, pickle relish, productions, and comparisons.
We tied together TV shows, and made plays after midnight in Hollywood.
The lazy chairs we sat in were stuffed with holes
steeped in deep conversation, facing each other in Harlem.
You were the ever-present guest of 5J on that 1-2-5
and walked the four flights up on that 1-3-9
paying no mind to my junk and gravity.

There was always a chicken in your bag and a play on your mind.
You quenched friendship with kikis and cocktails,
wandering over bridges,
wondering and gossip, buttery shrimp,
love and protection, praying for my husband to find me.
You were drunk at our wedding (reality).
Yes, you were drunk
and everyone knew
and everyone saw you.

You carried a tube of mustard into the movies with us
without explanation.
What was the fight about that day?
A fight at Magic Johnson over your weird mustard.
A fuss at BBQs.
I remember leaving you there in the dark
nervous about your hilarity
nervous about you toppling over and landing on me.
I wondered about your tremors and gums
I saw your pain in the crack-lit glimpses allowed me
by my own stingy and tone-deaf self absorption

counting out each of the aspirin for you, giving you *half* in a plastic bag —
after all you had ever given me.

I asked you to pick up the Mountain Dew from the bodega.
It's not enough to say
I was perturbed by your jeans
hanging off your ass
the slit of butt crack
giving me face
over at the stove
the butter, the garlic
the shrimp you carried all the way from Brooklyn in your bag.
You made me garlic shrimp in butter sauce that night.

I refused to eat the French bread at first, watching my carbs.
Then I ate more than my fair share.
Toasted circles of buttery bread
I snuck into the kitchen past midnight to stuff in my mouth.

We were watching *Empire* reruns all night.
Cookie had done this and that
in potato- chip- ghetto- glamour.
We went crying over the beyond and the folks
already gone to there.
Your leg was in pain.
I offered you the futon to rest and *half* a tub of aspirin, stingy nurse.

I had no idea you were leaving me forever.
You pressed the wrong buttons on the remote
fucking up our television experience.
You were an expert on August Wilson for me those two days.
You slept on the futon.
You left in the morning,
texting me that you made it Home.

You watched the spectacle of heartache I offered endlessly
because you listened so well.
I luxuriated in your cackle and candor
greedy for your height
your version of intellect, your ears, your bohemia,
your light-skinned black mania

black Munstah
black Empire
black Shameless
black Thrones
black reality and know-how

You would delight in the growth of my gumbo
the color has grown dark and deep
you would love the butter inside
the green peppers I left at the store
the sales I find on shrimp
the crab boil my mother added
and how my love and bruh
drink half the pot
before it's done.

Slob and Tears

There was enough slob and tears
in the pot
from crying over my dead friend
that I didn't even need
to add butter.

 BLACK JELLY

Healing Looks Like A Mess

Healing
looks like
a mess.

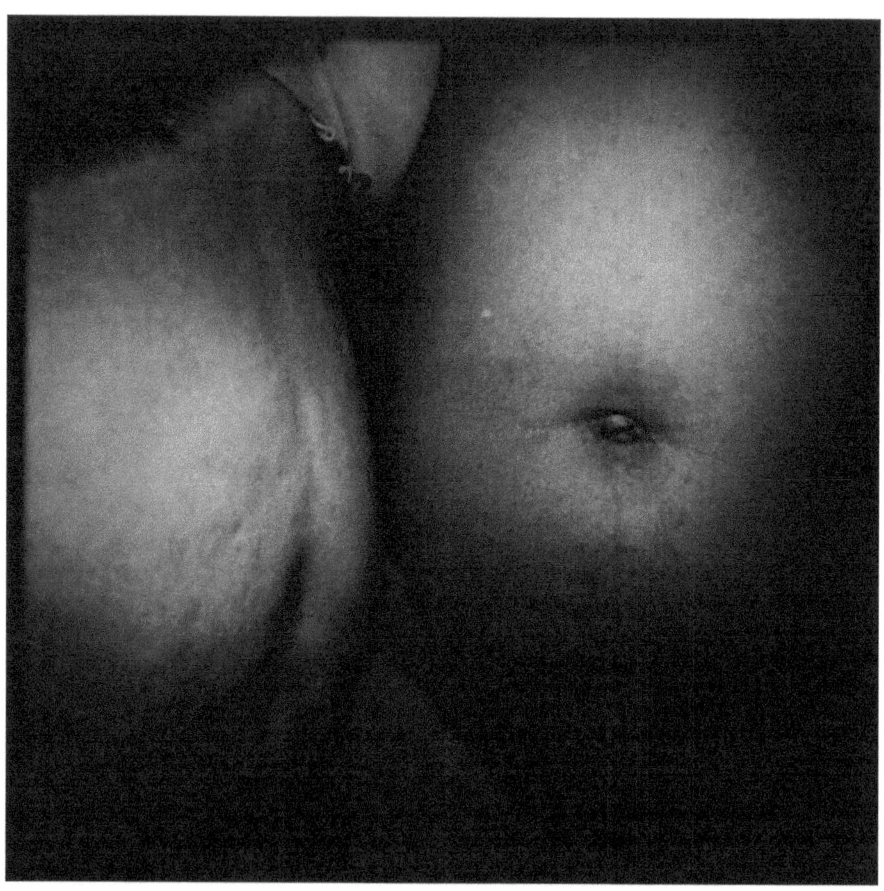

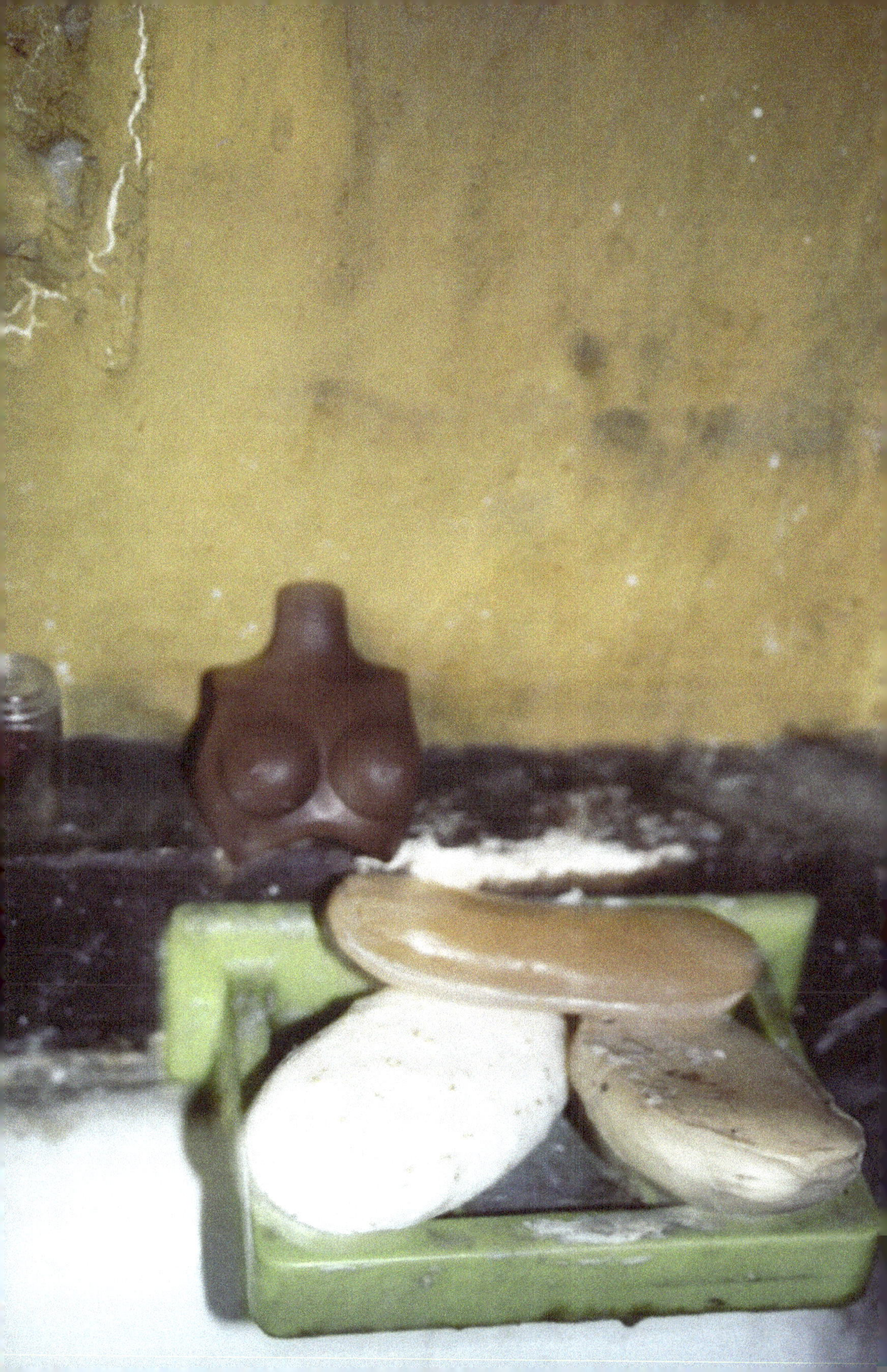

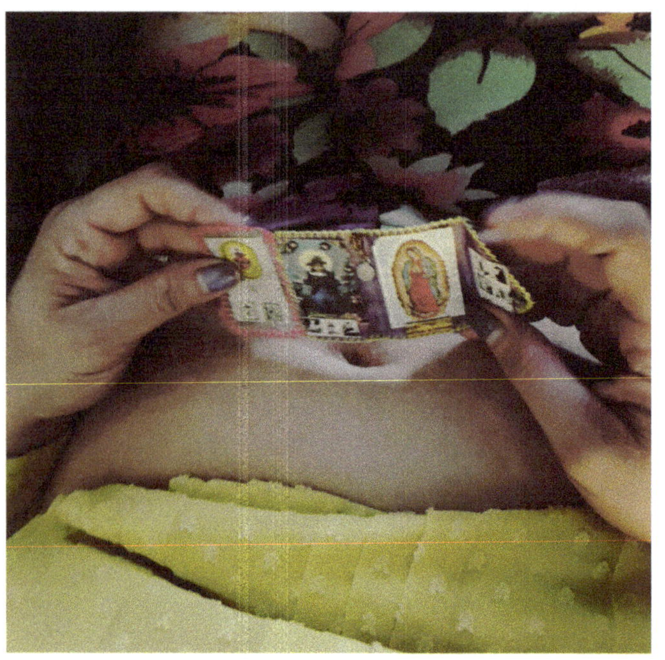
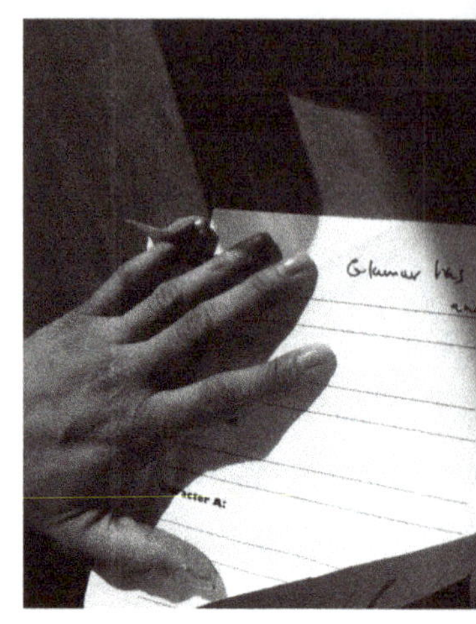
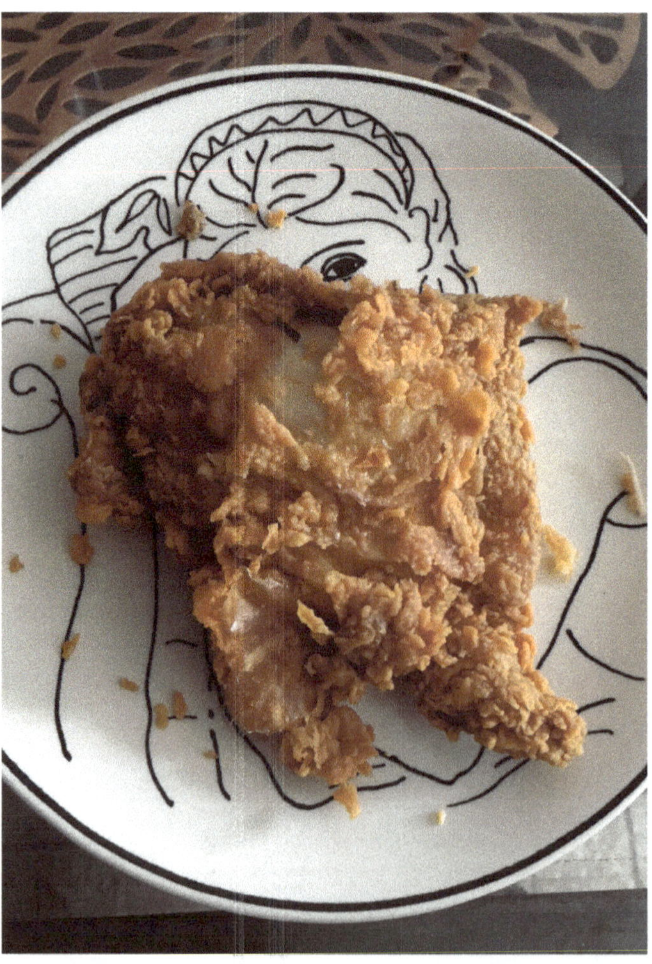
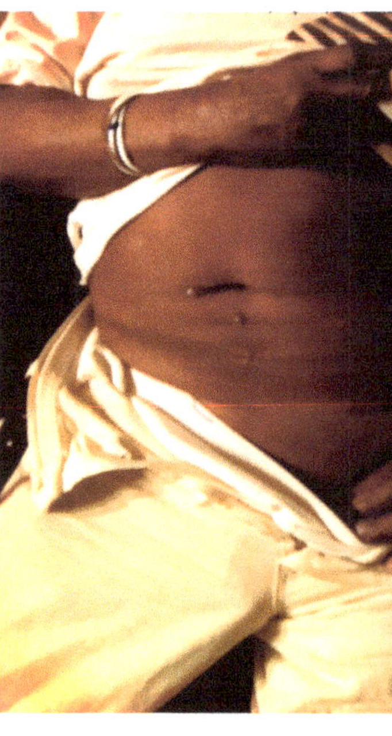
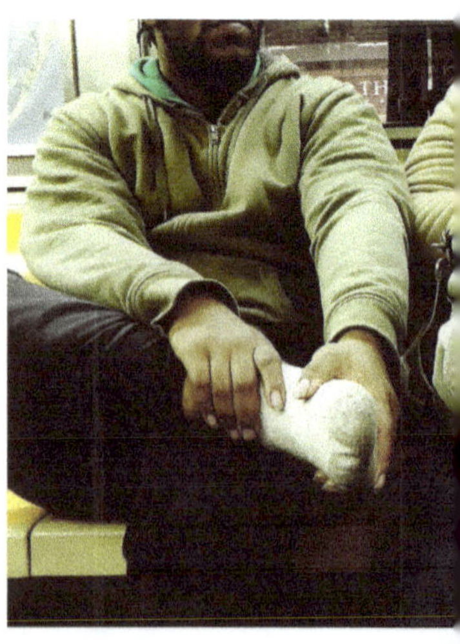

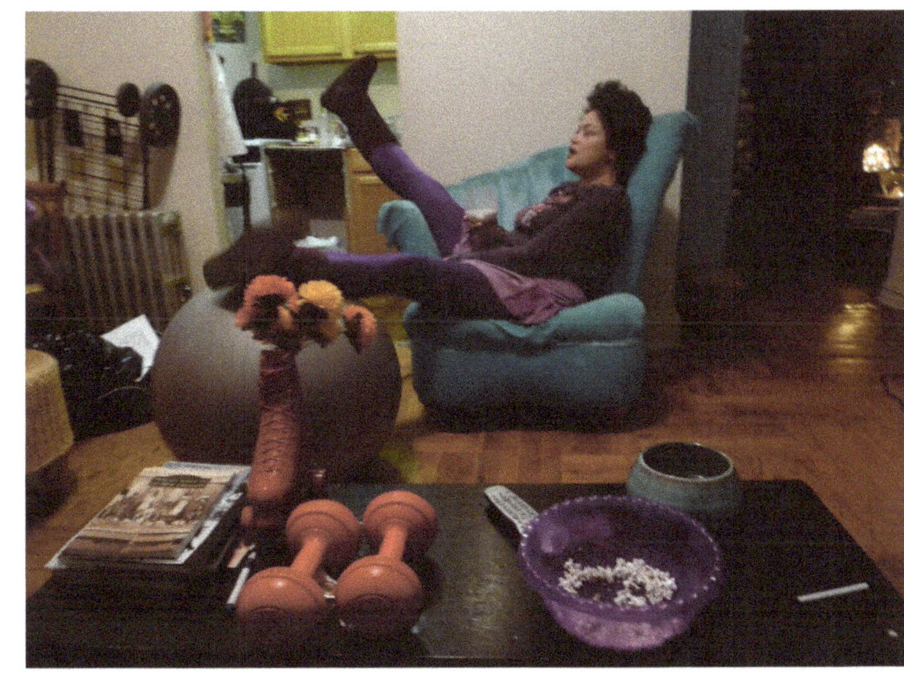
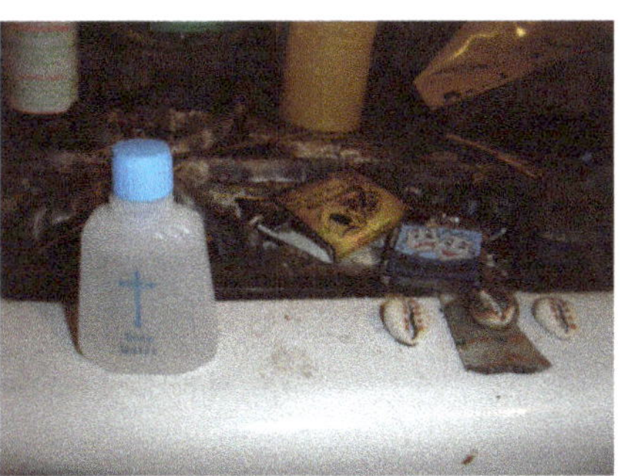
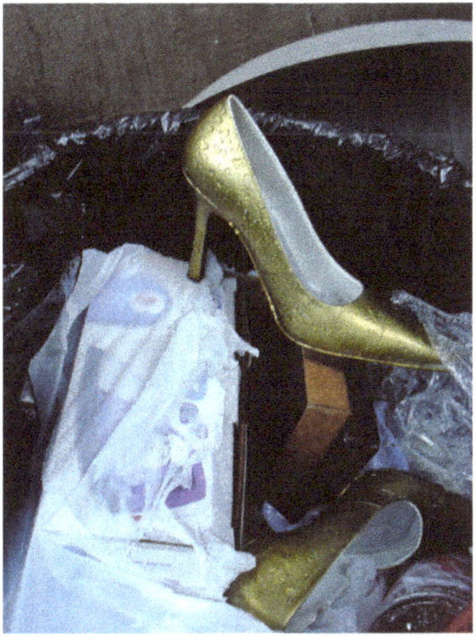
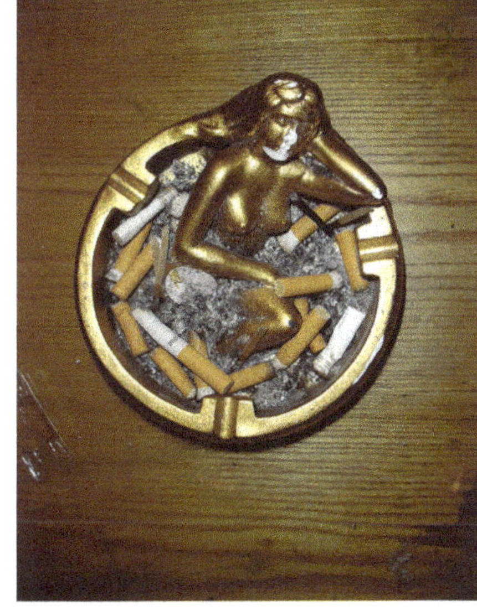
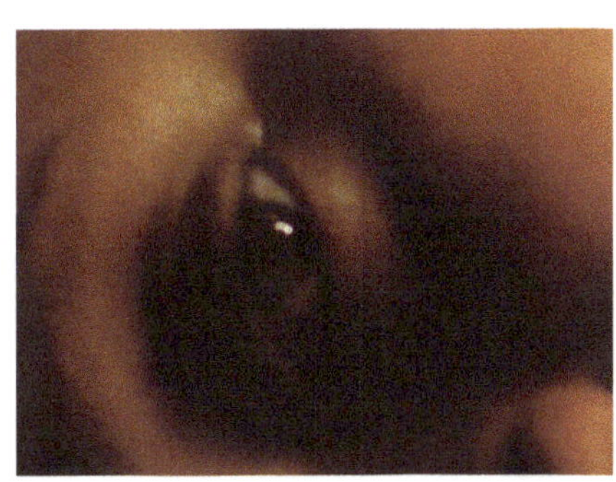
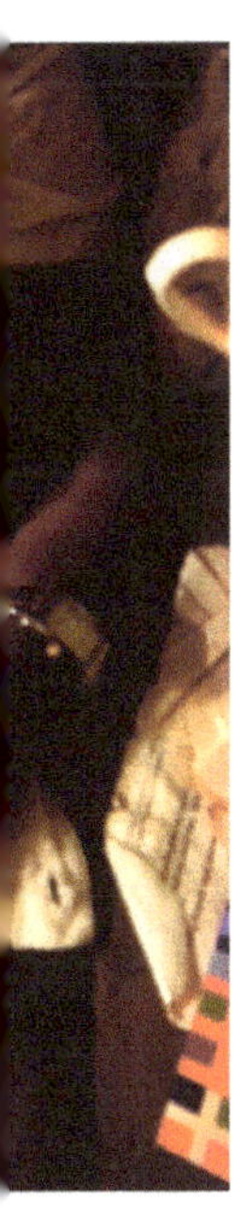
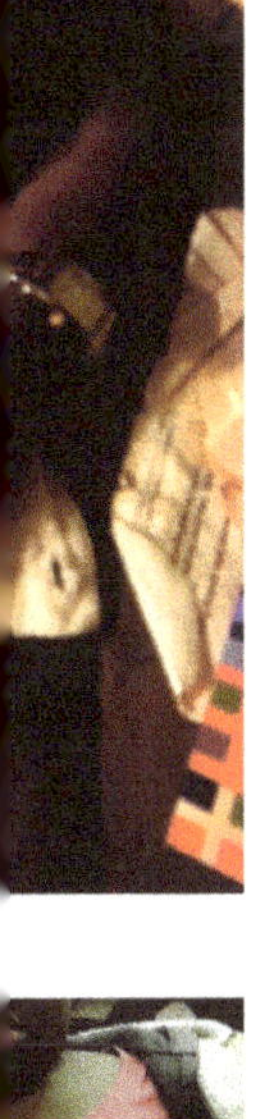
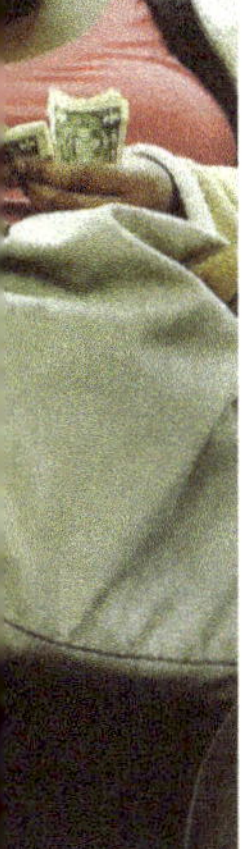

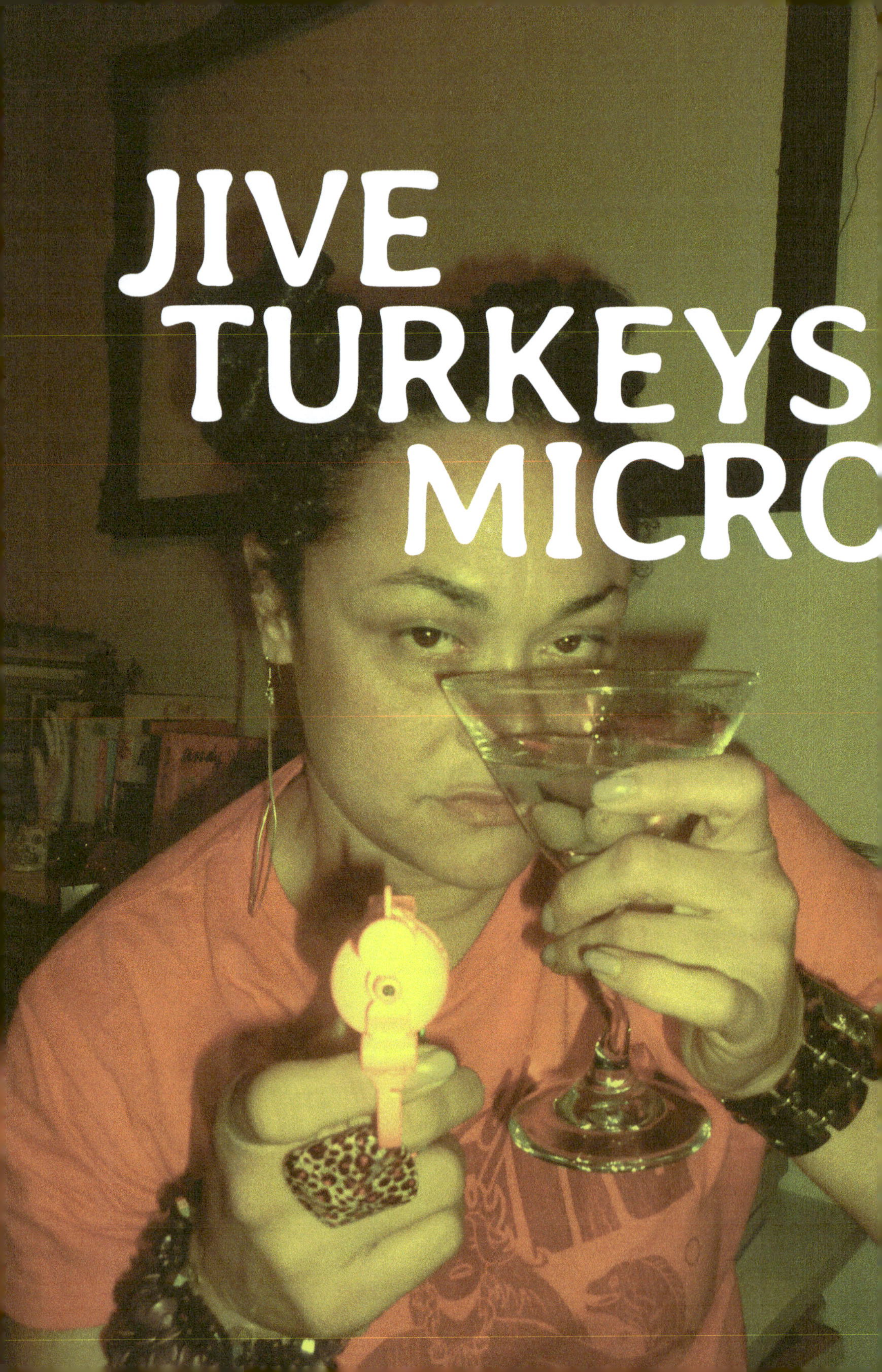

JIVE
TURKEYS
MICRO

3

AND WAVED BITCHES

Pelicans Handle Their Glasses

I. INJURY

I survived

        the heartache of Saturday

the clinking of forks

        the way pelicans

handle their glasses

        delicate
        people

scooping up the intimacy

        of meal and ceremony

occasion and dresses

        and every invitation

        that means something
        and nothing

Instead of dying,
like I thought I would,

looking up into
the white light of death

while   you   and fruit loop
        threw dirt on my head

        and salted
        the very wound
     you   compounded

sealing me further into that hot oven tomb
of St. Louis Number One

my name inscribed beneath my grandmothers
        Ethel and Virginia…

        killed by your injury.

II. APOLOGY

Instead of all that

I spent the morning
        ALIVE and breathing

        deep inside

Alicia Custer's apology   sunset dances   and Apache grandmothers

leaving the person I was
and the time
and the apology
not made on my behalf

        thinking of ways

        to forgive you
fit for sacred song
and psycho-soul analysis

leaving the present person
you cornered me into being

the one   you mugged of a friendship
the one   you stuffed into a suitcase and left at the airport
        with no destination or intention to return
no carry-ons
no companions

what a relief that Black Kettle says to send you a gift

the transformation   of anger
        into a blue paper package
        filled with a photo
        maybe some words
        maybe a picture of Black Kettle himself
        probably a rat, maybe a rosary

I'm not sure   what   to give   you

anymore.

III. MAUVE MOTH

Bitterness will shed
                                    its sin   like skin

no   butterfly   will   emerge

my biggest hope   is a flying mauve moth

                                            that circles up high

                                            catching your attention

its fleeting wings

                slipping through

                a hole   in your screen door

finding   a larger gush   of air somewhere

returning to
the oldest ancestor   in   me

that welcomes   the   love   inherited

by   seven   directions.

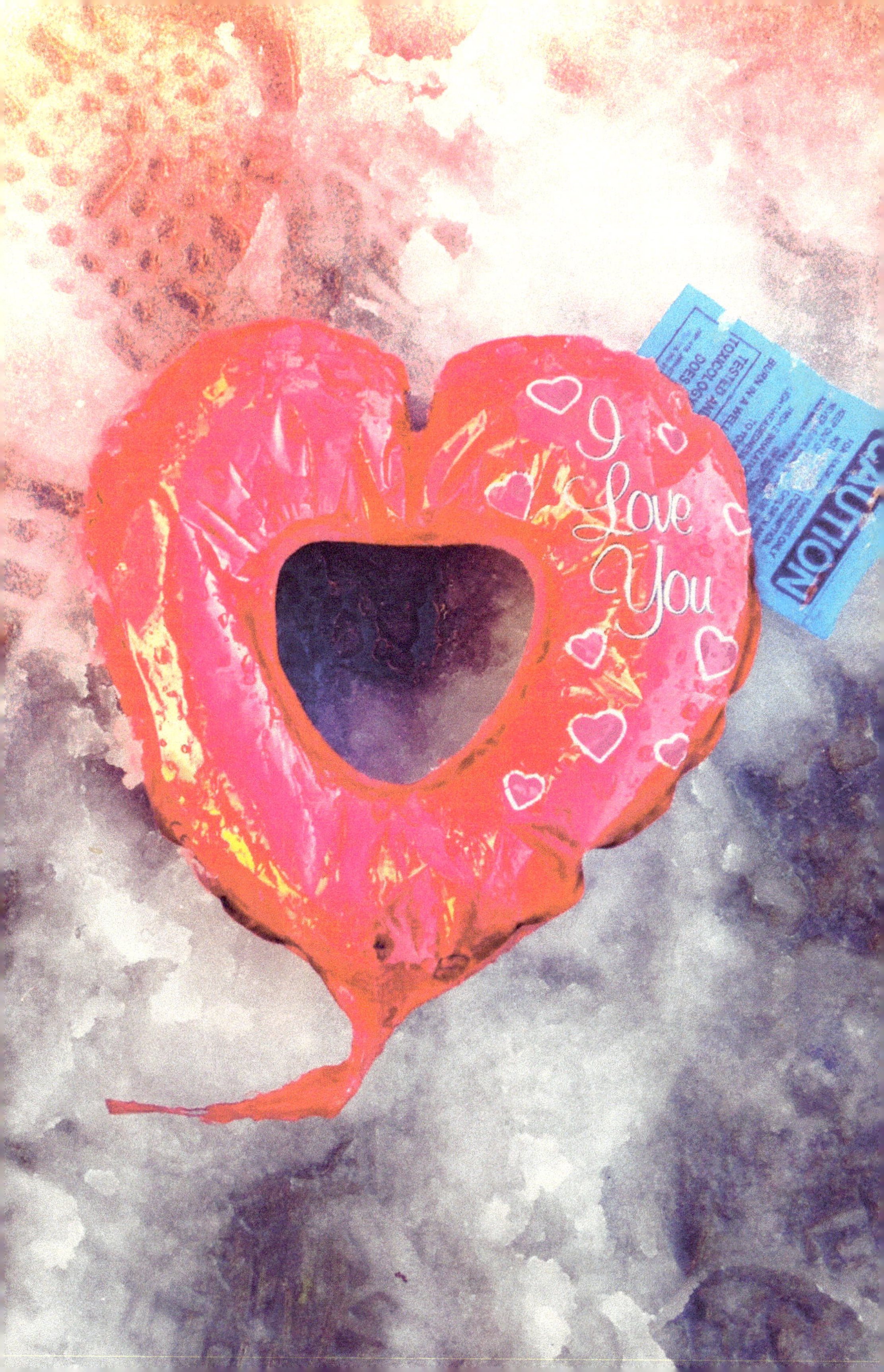
I Love You
CAUTION

Redboned Hot Comb

A place in a braid
                    a single strand
                    of red hair
                    is not the weave
                    that flies in the air
hair is my consolation
a sign of more
is not a haircut
a razor
is not blood or bleeding or needing.

The resemblance to skin is affectionate
and shaving cream in the sink.

The afro mixture   is black/ is negro   not creole in color
but bush   and dashiki   all together.

There is no gratitude   in weddings and cliques.
There can be breakages   in Creole loyalties.

There will always be a difference between

                                        nappy hair and high yellow

                                        beige translucent skin

                                        born brown

                                        bun brown

                                        brown

tresses needing a hot comb   redboned tomato

and the few that really roll carefree.

The severance chosen

will embarrass someone worse than me one day

I hope.

If lying is not natural, there is some use in letting go.

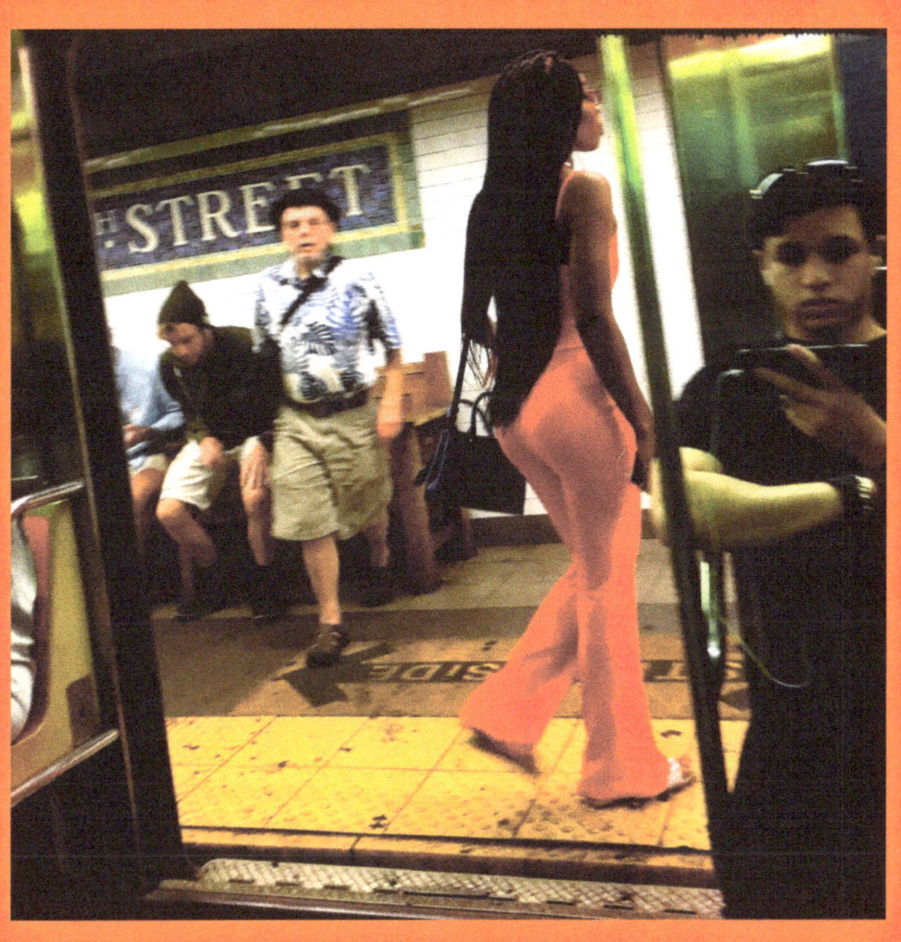
STREET

Jungle-Green Poet Verses
Well-Seasoned Poet

Older seasoned poet capped by younger poet,
she, green like jungle
her voice — loud, like lion-long
big booty, nostrils wide with youth, breathing like King Kong.

Tight pants holding in totally toned
big hips, doing dips, pokey lips
fake fingernails and fake finger tips.

Lips poking out with kiddy bubblegum tasting lip gloss
mmmmmmmmmmmmmmm
all the high school boys say when she walks in
mmmm they say.

She is a rainstick-shaker *pah pah pah* poetry maker
able to do cartwheels with her tight pungent vagina
spreading like a V
a spinning cycle of red ripe ovaries.

I am just dried-up blood in a wheelchair with grey hair.

She's got a name that sounds like she made it up —
Tiger Woman Womb, Toni Yoni Egg, Shaking Earth Tree,
when I'm just plain ol' Melanie with an i.e.

She's the kind of woman who'd take over a drum circle
rum pah pah pum flipping around in nature
afro-poofs of hair screaming from her underarms
just one of her youthful charms.

She smells like the same patchouli oil I sported out when *I* was twenty two.
I teach a poetry class. She teaches a poetry class, too.
(At the same school, fool.)
I don't know *why* she was hired, since I was never fired — *ahhhhhhh.*
Enough of a stage to share.

On the microphone at the student showcase presenting the poetry projects of
our prodigies, this is what we do:

Congratulations to my students:
we studied Mary Oliver's Wild Geese,
William Cars Wimmlins, I mean, William Carlos Williams,
This Is Just to Play, I mean This is Just to Say,
Tyki Gynovammi, I mean, Nikki Giovanni's
Ego's Ripping, sorry, Tripping,
the poetry of Major Fraction, I mean I'm so sorry, Major Jackson
and Where I'm From by Willie Pernomo,
oh no... oh no...oh no, I mean Willie Perdomo.

Oh, No!

I'm so sorry I'm stuttering
getting the names all wrong, muttering
because my allergies are so bad
and my lips, they are stuck together
and the salivas in the corners of my mouth
are fighting to stay alive
'cause I'm so old, and I'm so jive
and my mouth is so arid-dry from some
sort of hormonal imbalance
or diabetic episode that's happening to me right now
I don't know how
in this moment in front of all of you — eh, uh,
dealing with such dehydration and other such occupations
that happen in this latter station of, oh, my, just, so please, please
just enjoy these deep and bountiful expressions from our troubled youth,
our quite troubled youth, Ah — Thank you.

Bridesmaid jungle young green poet, grabs the mic
does an African dance and a cartwheel to the stage
a pungent pussy whirl that shows her age:

Hello, Pow Boom.
Hello, Pow Boom.
My booty's big.
Hello, Bam, Pow, Boom.
I know, you can't take your eyes off of it.
Hello, Bam, Pow, Boom.
I'm so fresh and so urban.
Hello, Pow, Boom, Bam
and you love me so much.
I talk New York City like a black girl and have so much to prove.
You are brilliant.

Hello, Pow, Bam, Boom.
You will be the change of the world!
You are the change of the world!
And I am so significant because I'm the first to ever tell you this!
And I am here to make old poets feel older
and replaceable like vases
and mark the wide contrast between the wrinkles on our faces!
I have no lines, I'm just young and big and super fine!
I make big-young-wide woman faces with no fear
of wrinkles while I'm here!
And, thank you —
thank you, thank you: for the many, many, many years I have reached out and
become so close to each and every one of you and each and every one of
the chairs and classrooms and desks, and each and every one of the teachers
here who I eat snacks with and lunch with yeah, yeah, yeah, yeah and we go
on vacations together to the beach in Boom Pam Pow bikinis,
yeah, yeah, yeah!

I go back into my brain thinking of how insane it is
that she knows all the teachers but me
and we both teach poetry!
And I do feel some kind of way about that
because I'm older and because writers normally like each other
and respecting the space and elders and woman and culture
and yada, yada, YADAAAAA!
I've been teaching poetry for over 20 YARS
and I've been teaching poetry for twenty Muther-fucking YARS...
so long that I can call poetry, 'purratree,'
and I can call years, 'YARS!'

I am an institution.
I am a pen of passing on and history.
I instituted all the tricks you think are slick as if you are so novel.
Poetry video, who made poetry video?
Landed students on the moon?
Who landed students on the moon?
So young! So obtuse!
Never even bothering to see my season, my style, my older stroke,
or just even saying, *'hello?'*

Jungle young continues:
I call my students by their rap names:
Violeta B, Candy Lee, Super Tee say your poetry for me!
Pooka pooka, pooka, pooka, scraH-scraH-scratch!

You make me feel so comfortable and safe here!
And I'm never going to leave this school
because I am no fool
and I am here to rob
the old poetry lady's job!
Boop boop boop ta boop ta boop boop!

I grab the mic:
What? Well, I feel so safe and at home with my poetry students here
that I keep a sleeping bag in my classroom
in case I want to spend the night and dream up lesson plans about poetry
and poetry and poetry and poetry and poetry
and Langston Hughes and Claude McKay
and Shakespeare and Gwendolyn Brooks, and John Donne —
old time poets like that, Old Fashioned!

Jungle young grabs the mic:
my poetry students are so deep
they got blood coming out of they arms spilling from they veins
onto their papers
because I empassion them with each and every letter they write
and they pour themselves out on the pages of my pages that I made
with my bare hands, from trees!
We are blood bound by my fly poetry class!

I grab the mic:
my students are so deep,
and I'm so hip and cool and you love me so much at this school,
that I bring them to the tattoo parlor down the block
and we get tattoos of our poems on our thighs and faces — so there!

Jungle young takes the mic:
Bitch, I ain't going nowhere, this is my home.
This is my family.
I'm manipulating this situation like family does, hear?

I take the mic: *Bitch, I met my man here.*

Jungle: *All these 'bitches,' that ain't cool or PC, especially not in poetry.*

Me: *Bitch, even PC is way younger than me!*

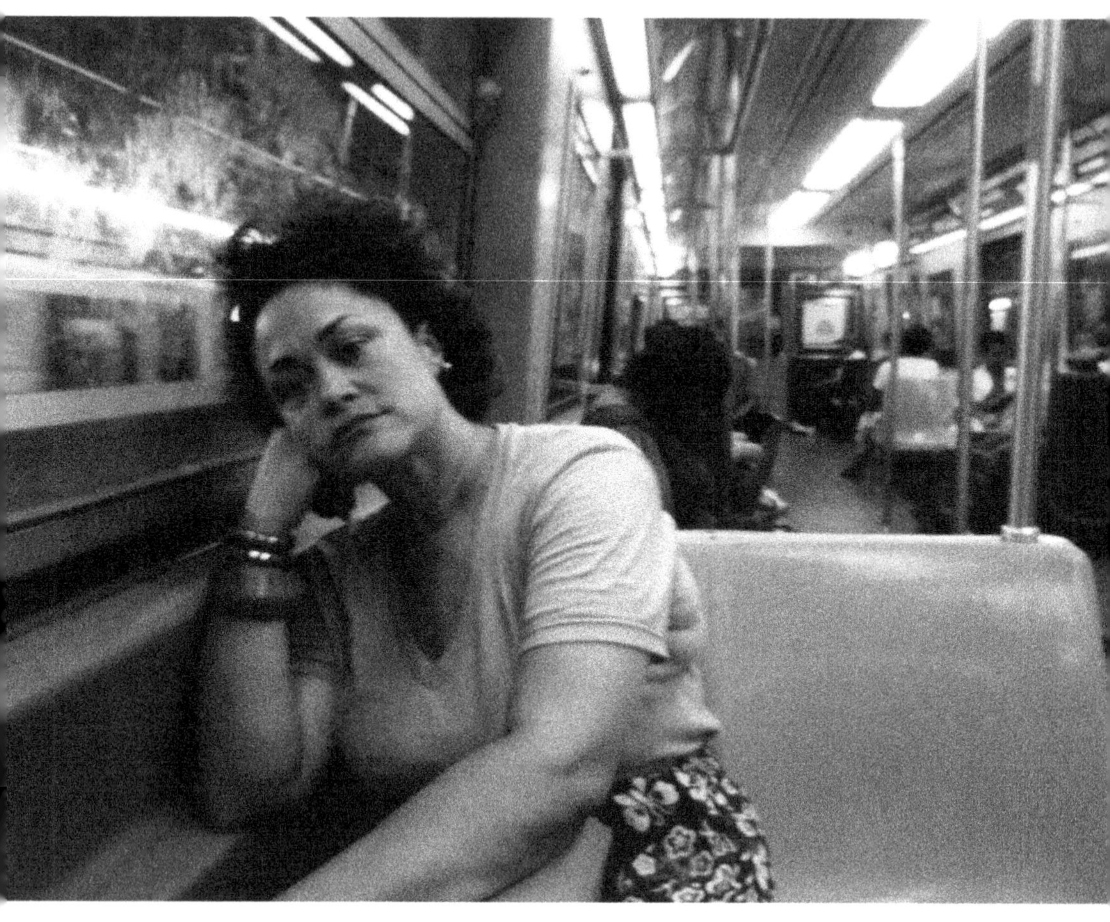

BLACK JELLY

I'm so old
the way I grab onto the subway pole
and shove my belly up and go slowwwwww
crankety crankety crank to the side
a poet stuck in time,
but still, I rhyme!
A pause, a pout, a pain
just a few years from a cane
next time you see me
a most abrupt pee pee
and I'll bee bee
rolling around Key Food in a machine,
this is but a dream.

Thank You for Not Being an Uppity Negro

Thank you for not being an uppity negro
holding a fig leaf
tight in your cinnamon-bun brown ass
holding up your middle-brown nose to the people
who live beneath rotting blankets below the underpass
'cause you so upperclass

I wouldn't want to live there either though
close to the bugs
split-stretched flimsy black plastic bags
used for too many moves
junk falling out
cardboard boxes
fleas, eyes, reminders of who's left to not love you
vulnerable to cops and cars and vagrants and judgements and attacks.

Thank you for grimacing when I said,
What's happening, Man?! like the other B L A C K S
clutching your pearls
afraid that the next word out of my mouth might be

D Y N O M I T E

JJ and Good Times
cracklings and pig lips

                greens and high fives
                all   the   way   LIVE

Glad you opened the door to a room of books you kept me from,
Mr. Harriet Tubman of the not-North.

And then you became silly.   I noticed your slight accent.

Must be mixed with a Spaniard somewhere?
With your ascot and wavy hair?

Or are you so country that you
swallow the ends of your words like a banjo twang?

Eating pickles in the heat
dipped in red kool-aid and Tang Tang Tang?

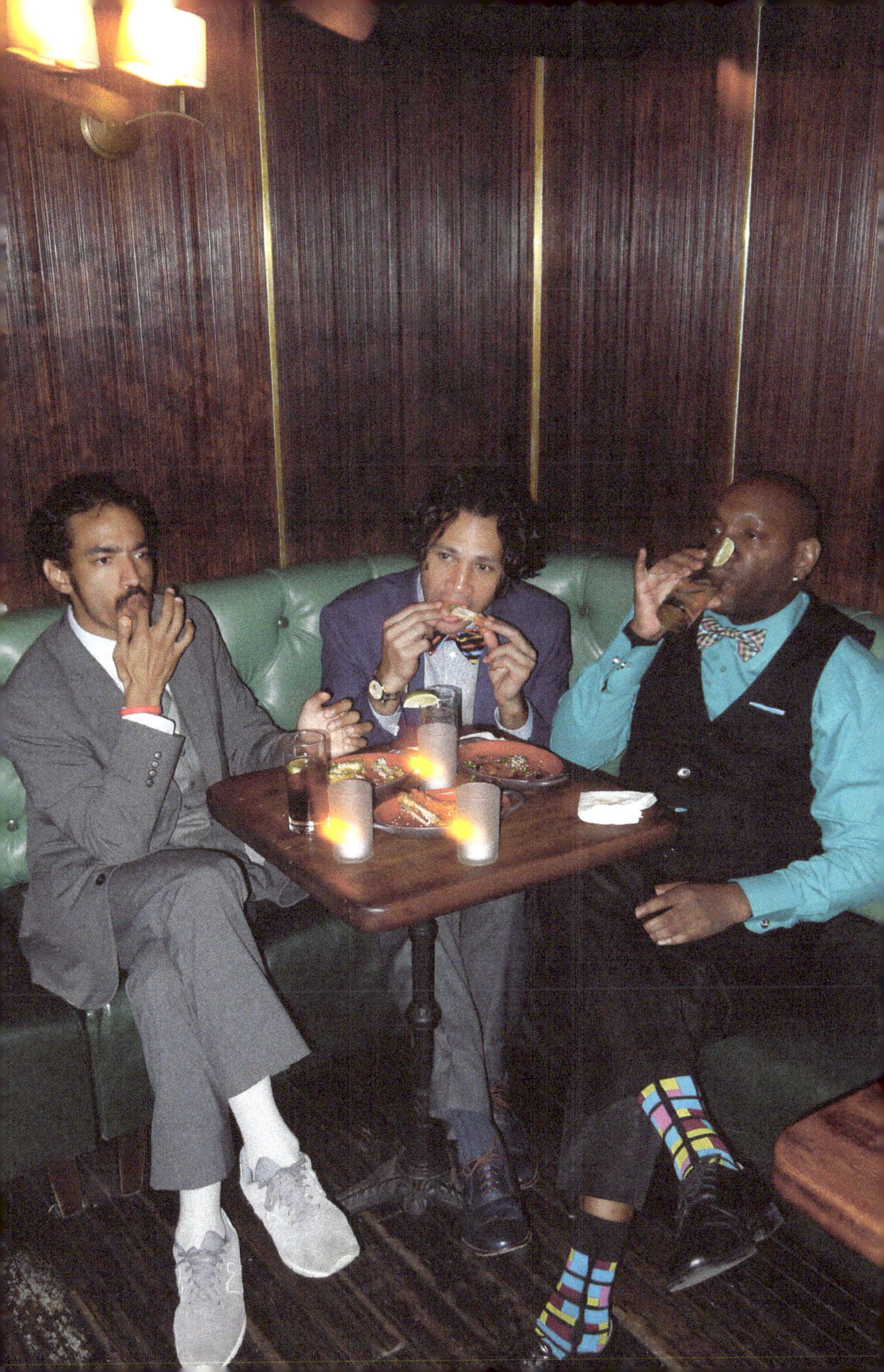

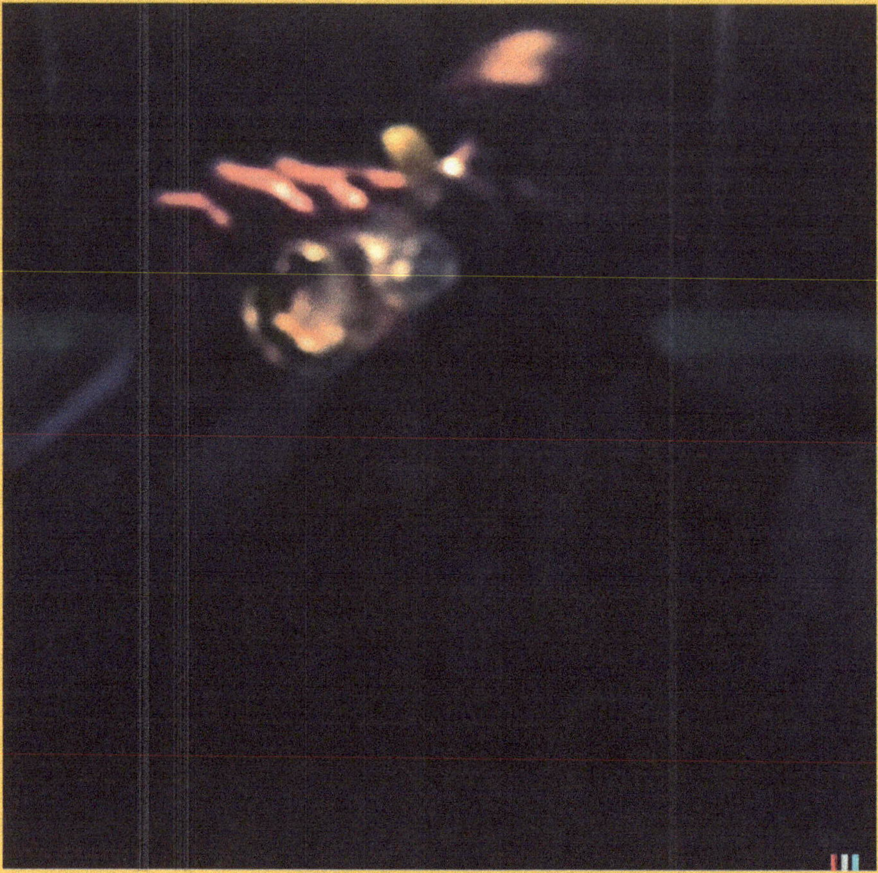

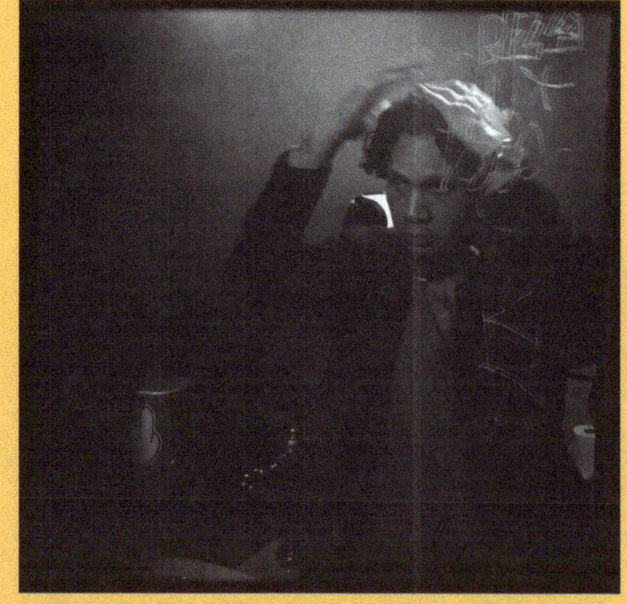

Looking like a refashioned Langston Hughes
trying not to be Prince
in your preppy uppity brown boarding school shoes.

Grown man in a suit
a mirror
where you undress
revealing the brown
and its stress
living to impress
bearing the same heaviness

of   B L A C K   MAN   WORLD:

      oh, puzzling conundrum of mystery,
      sweet soft bed of brown lips,
      Old Spice, dress socks, ham-hocks
      the bricks you carry in your backpack
      the hope of rhymes and pork rinds
      or no pigs on your plate
      a good grind for a slow drag at a Saint Aug dance
      the crawfish you brung in a paper bag
      dripping with enigma on a bus for us

How   do   you   work?

      the powerhouse of your nonchalance
      the way you went to jail that time
      you played my body like a bass
      the fiddle I became in your fingers
      the collard greens you made for me
      dripping in lime-colored grease
      surrounded by turkey necks
      manning the bbq in slippers
      sweet sauce handed down
      lotion on your ashy man feet,
      dirty hearts, card games, stories of glories
      baseball diamond fights in red sand
      your brown arms hanging out the window
      of an old burgundy car with the top down
      sun heating up seats and scorching thighs
      that burn for husbands
      each thump of bass a beat of promise
      for breathing

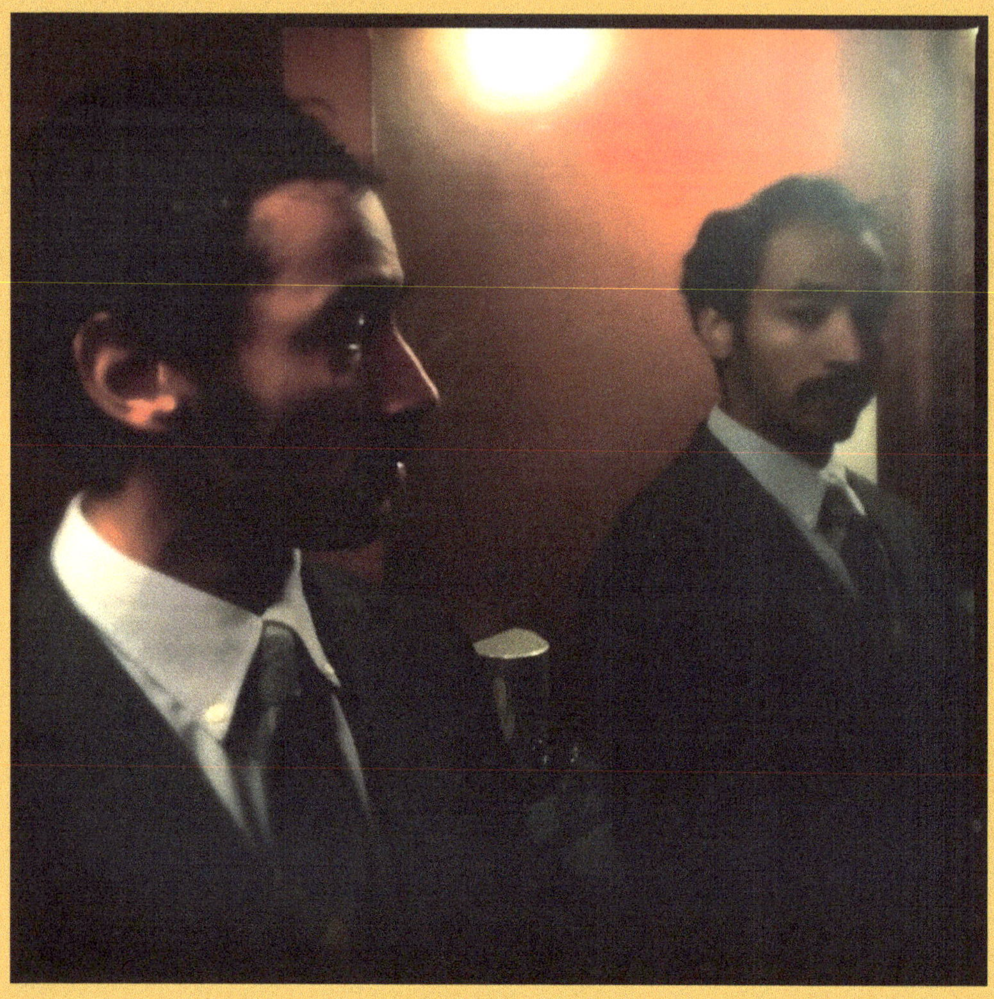

Grown man in a suit

a mirror
where you undress

revealing the brown
and its stress

living to impress
bearing the same heaviness

of   B L A C K   MAN   WORLD

the mystery that is not me

the why

you   wear   a tie

while you try

not   to   die.

Two More Cents

Hot sex
lick buns
boiled eggs
petrified branches
nests, twigs
between thighs

grind grunt
pressure cooker
rub a
dub dub
wash tits
in tub

ovulation conversation
will turn
winter into
longer winter
talk less
eat less

Your baby
will keep
avoiding you
if you
don't do
prescribed chanting

fertile wombs
are open
call life
don't drink
don't smoke
marijuana, mama

jerk kids
shit on
poetry lessons
hurt poet's
too sensitive
feelings, fuck!

Dude, if
your bagel
crumbs or
coffee spills
on me
you're dead

Stop slurping
in my
ears. Stop
smelling like
you're drunk
on the q5.

I hate
strangers much
of the
time.
Messy mouths
knocking legs

go away.

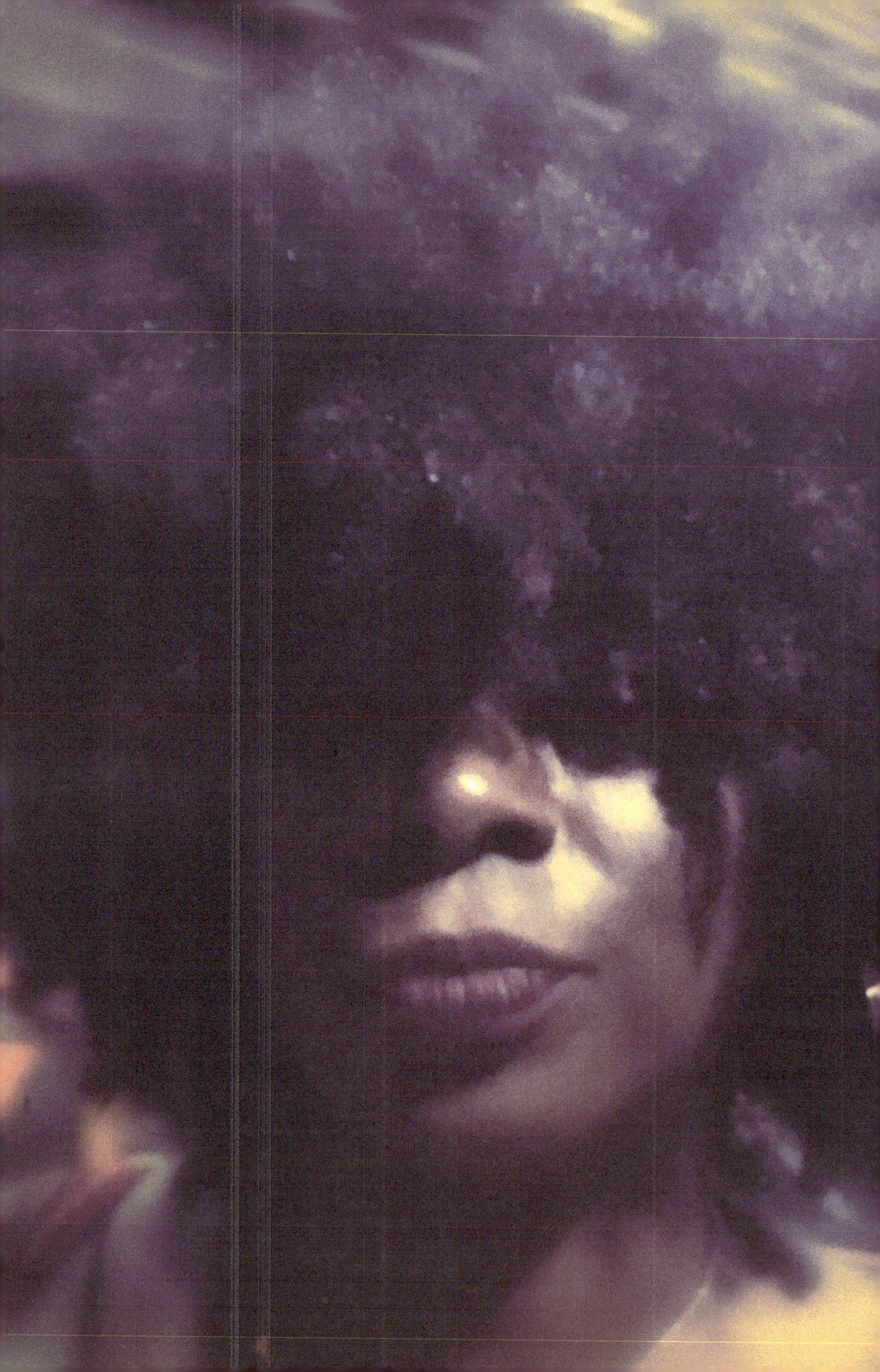

KIN
KINK
CONK

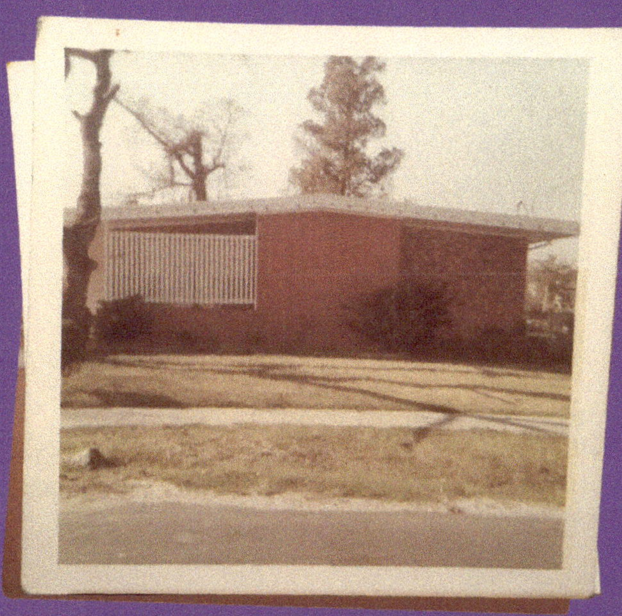

Relations

Prissy hands mopped with chicken blood
washing the good parts off
in the sink
while I think
reserving

breast   leg   thigh
for something special
my   *oh*   *my*

gutting out the bird
the gamey gunk left smelling in the proverbial plastic bag

I will make this rare bird taste good for company

while ogling
my hot pink glitter
gel manicure

        I will cook him
        I will bite him
        rub him with red pepper and oil

        I will spend quality time
        with this fowl of Key Food
        wrapping him in foil

        ingesting him
        he will become me
        this chicken is kin

as far as blood goes
it comes   it goes   it flows

the kite in the sky
is my cousin
        the dream going by
        is my mother

the darkest days of unbelievable sin
is one sister's brother
and that is why she mothers another

we are related by string bean casseroles
stories told
days spent at Money beach

we are related by hooks, by Heaven and its good company
by Spades games, by sunburns, by guilt, by obligation

we are related by time
peach cobblers, turned corners
walls, roles, performances, delayed planes

we are related by mess
a yellowing wedding dress
from the fifties

a marriage gone bad   a marriage gone good   a soul mate

all the conundrums we never got over
the consequences of a blind date
therapy, pills, pain, weight gain
the things we don't say

we are related by bloody gums, a tooth gone loose
bad credit, hair in the sink, secrets, sucrets
the orange-stains of mercurochrome
mayonnaise on the bread, finding grandma dead
whippings, a baby in the basket sent down the river
Moses, a sick doctor, a crucifix, a mind melting away

we are related by hopping in the back of the maroon Pontiac —
driving days to Denver, ice machines at hotels
Schwegmann's bags and book covers

heart attacks
diapers and shit

funk and fights
plasma and kin

fried chicken skin
the blood within

My Pudenda Is Not a Mother

My pudenda did not give birth.
Neither did I.
We do not want to walk outside today.
People will keep saying,
Happy Mother's Day to me.
We did not push out
any person formed on the inside of my womb.
No one delightful came from inside of me
and into the world.
Pudenda gave birth to no dragons either.
No oxygen shared, no tiny hands involved with placenta.
No nourishment.
No tit spills.
No cartwheels at camp.

Each time semen
came into our being,
it was washed away like fish smell
and had no utility
and did not blossom
and needed no baby clothes
no nickname
and never was picked up
or coddled or said a word.

Every Mother's Day
Pudenda thinks of dying.
Me too.
I don't know
drowning in a pool
doused by amniotic sac
hanging ourselves with an umbilical cord
made out of papier mache.
I fall deep into a day of tears
even though I should be swimming in sunshine
roller skating away from the day
brushing off the biblical birth pains
of every child's skull
pushing far out
to get out get out get out of
my pudenda.

I can see
the hard work
ahead of us
oh, barren day of fecund debris
the imagined mother of another dimension
my water breaks
the brutal blur
that will not be answered by any face

I can see
the hard work we will never do

how I mourn each period
dodged drudgery
crying when I see dark blood

walking like an unperson
through the sidewalks of flowers
unaddressed to me nonchalantly
Pudenda gets nada neither.
How selfish
how selfish
how selfish of us
how self absorbed
my own wet freckles
salty and pregnant
with rebirth and redirection
Pudenda goes on, expecting a shower gift from Macy's.
I artificially inseminate the moment
with something more worthy to talk about.
My pudenda did not give birth.

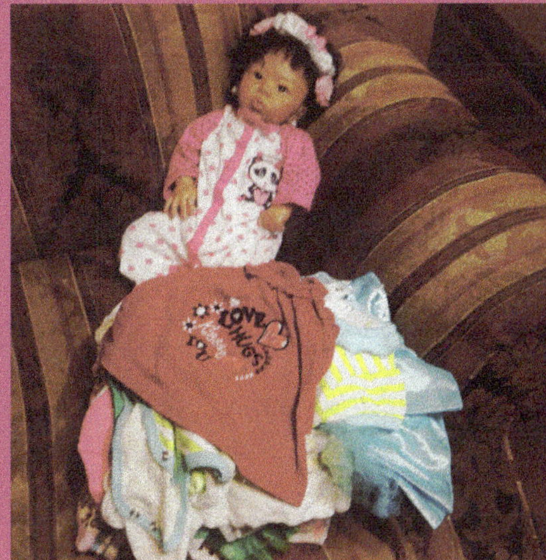

Two Cents/Promised Theological Essay

Perplexed by
clear differences
between sisters
Martha, Mary
Bible stars
doing chores

Did Jesus
know the
prep time
necessary for
hosting himself
and crewe?

I'm always
anticipating visions
what's next
quantities, debts
junk hunks
job snobs

the nerve
of Mary
to chill.
My own
sister watches
me lay

back beneath
my mother
forget dishes
neglect floors
bask, relax
leaving home

to roam
prodigal ways
piggy needs
smoking weeds
fat hen
broke again

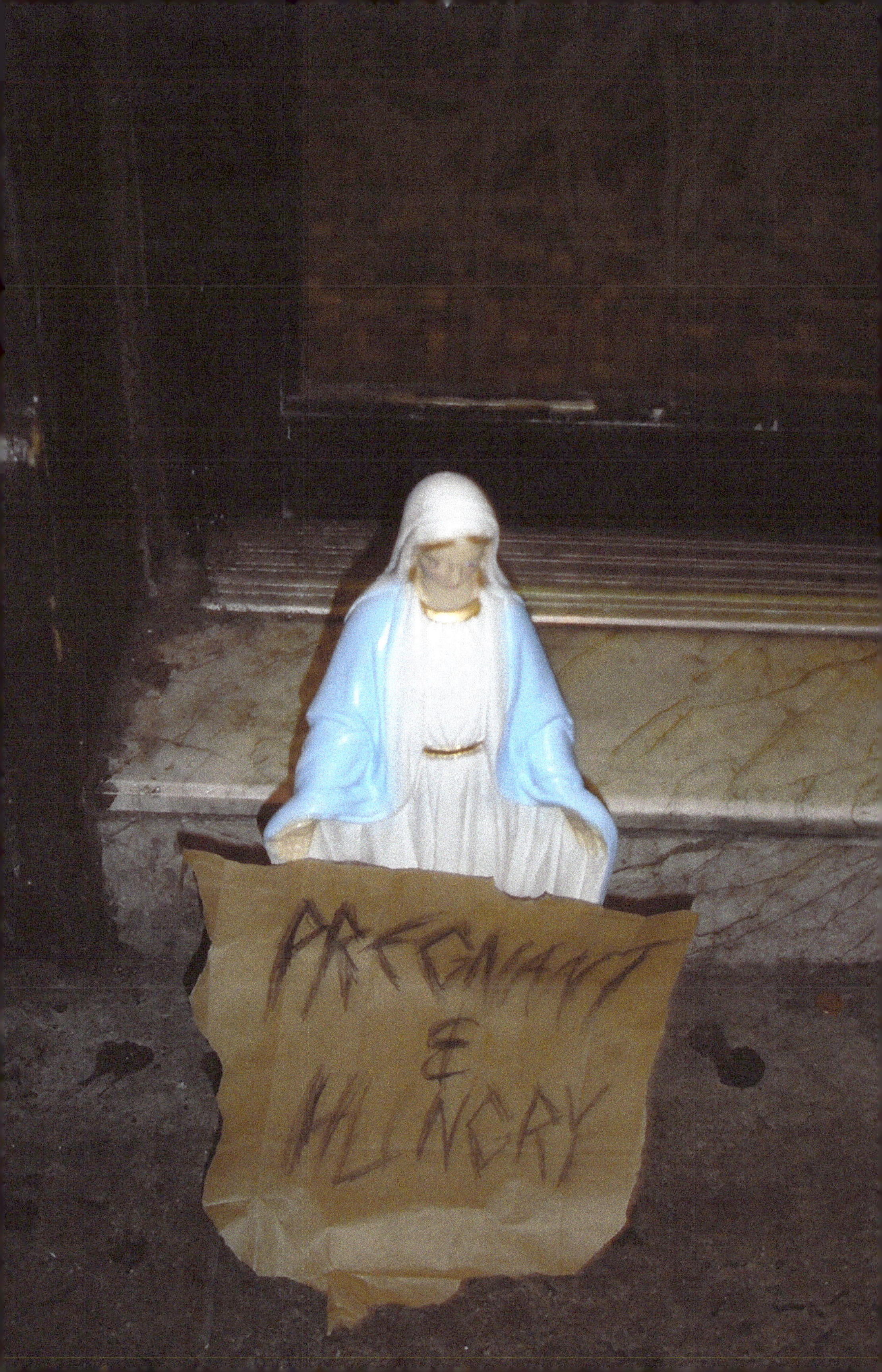
PREGNANT
&
HUNGRY

Martha stays
respects days
knows time
never whines
only nags
lazy rags

who chill
leave spills
don't seem
to see
messiness left
for thee, gee.

Martha groans
bulging discs
in spine
bending all
the time
picking up

shit, folding,
cleaning, scolding
Mary gets
good part
conversation starts
puts down

the mop
dances free
hip hop
meets God
spends time
sitting, chit-chatting
ha-ha-ing with
Lord, who
lets Mary
do nothing
no worrying
about a

thing. Ching
plates, shoes
dough, how
the night
will go,
the flow

she won't
know. Martha
will carry
all that
goes nary
sit with

stress, irons
Mary's dress
cleans mess
worries much
needs touch
no rest

while Mary
keeps the
best — ?

Brother in Three Bites

I. Brother wiped several snakey smiles
off of slick Southern suited salesmen
with one *fuck you* and a slammed door
at the car dealership in front of me and mamma.
We gave them back the Altima
they sold us like fish-eyed fools and cobras.

II. Brother builds pralines well, cooks jambalaya
that tastes smokey-familiar, coon-ass-tough in the backyard,
plays piano inherit of Olga-Rose, will gank you at Scrabble,
build you a table, a bench, a bed, scratches a back with sleek
technique and complicates notions of blackness while reading
Cornel West and playing or not playing golf at the same time.

III. Brother shared my father's cold dead body
with me before it was embalmed.
We were all alone in some hospital room.
I grazed my hands across my father's refrigerated chest
before I'd never be able to touch him again.
Brother just touched him real quick —
brave and scared like the cadaver we loved might bite.

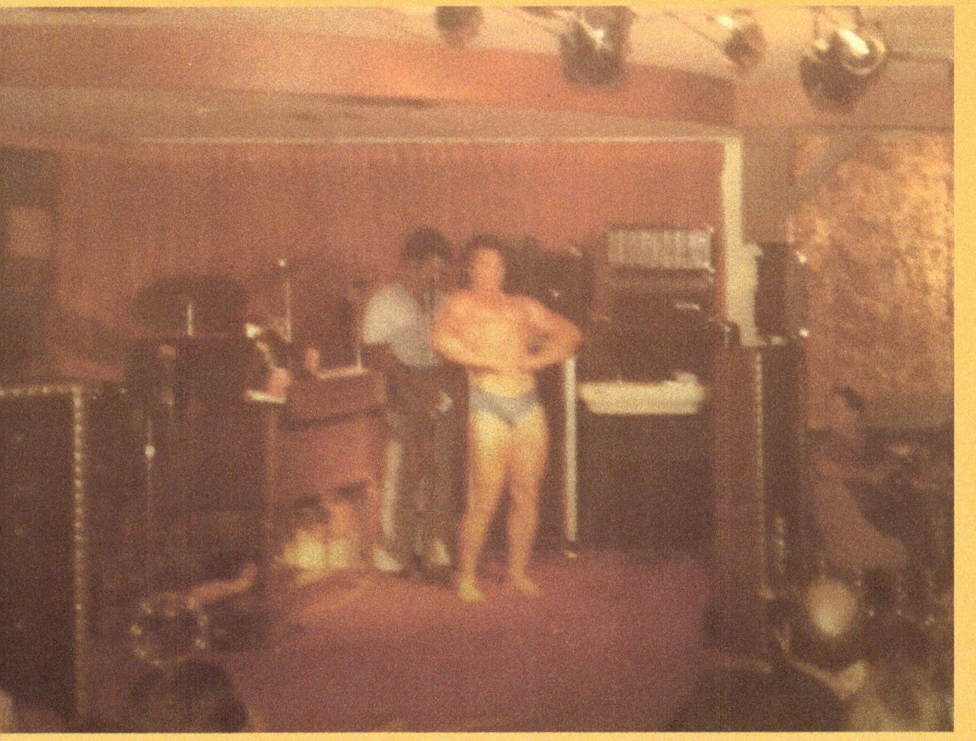

Parrain's Prayer

Parrain took his role as my Godfather very seriously.
Oh, the times he must have mentioned me to Jesus.
How many times his cerebrum counted the thought of me to Mary —
his fingers passing over a plastic bead
no bigger than a holy watermelon seed
over and over and over again.

Maps of prayer, roads to Medjugorje.
Parrain loved the rosary
and said one dressed in black and gold before the Saints game in some
hospital close to the time spelled out as the end for him.
(Only God knows when the end's at hand.)

Uncle Parrain didn't talk so much, but he said all of his Hail Marys
and uttered half-boldly in a voice shaking from passion and devotion
deep inside his old Creole man self
white hair pointing a shaking finger at my carefree consort,
"He's a man of the rosary."
I poked out my lips and raised my eyes,
"For real?" with salt.
My doubt wasn't beyond Uncle's consideration, even with him so sick.
It took everything in him to say, "You'll see."

In a matter of minutes, my-ever-prayed-for-Agnostic-love
returned from the bathroom
and repeated Mary's prayers with these very specific participants:

> Uncle, Parrain, a man who told me I was never too old to get pregnant
> and pounded his knee with laughter, cracking himself up, blowing a
> wow-filling joy into his own belly over how fine his wife still was at
> seventy-eight years old,

> and his sister, my Mother, daughter of God, Algiers rosaries sanctified
> by her leadership, history and ancestors on her side, long time prayers,
> true believer, Holy Water stations in every room, each Sunday marked
> for Mass and a stack of prayers heavy like a loaded brick of holiness
> said every day from the lazy chair, Steve Harvey silently hosting the
> Family Feud just a lit image and noise over and yonder, and

> Auntie, fox of the family, bedside with a smile, wise counselor with a
> vision and class, a dreamer, good with a weed whacker, loyal member
> of every church, married to Uncle, and great at Spades and Bid Whist.

We murmured rosaries and sounded like waves of familiar rhythms
sonic to soothing, trying to concentrate hard on God.

Mama called on my skeptical Love to lead:

He stumbled over prayers
and caught snags at grace and the Lord being with thee
and my aunt and uncle who saved me for my entire life
from right across the street, leaning over their fence
a yard of buried dogs and histories
a life of birthday cakes with he and Auntie as my closest guests
pork chops to share on top a tin bin and paper towels with grease and TV.
They saved him too:
They gave him the right place and prayer and he kept moving in the ritual.
Reluctant Agnosticism losing to impassioned entanglement in a family,
moment pulling hard on spontaneity and honoring roots and ties.

I cried, I cried, I cried, so hard, Lord!
Salty tears plopping out my eyes with joy and sadness
like river water churning from the Natchez
the moment cast with a most
recherche ensemble of players
Uncle, Aunt, Mama, Husband
Virgin Mary, a beginning, an ending
Saints won, Saints lost
candle wax escaping visibility
while Parrain moved from this dimension
and on to the next.

Daddy

He worked at the post office and wore suits.
He owned no underwear, only boxers.
He was an accountant with excellent handwriting.
He was precise.

Daddy had smooth hands and nails that were perfectly manicured.
Daddy drove a baby-blue Volkswagen that he parked on our lawn.
Daddy was a Bonhomme Douze in a social club.
Daddy owned art and photographed Mardi Gras on Bourbon Street
with a 35-millimeter camera he was proud of.

Daddy had artist friends that gave him paintings —
one that looked like an insula of the future on burnt orange canvas.
Daddy was cool.
Daddy had stacks of magazines hiding at the top of his closet,
a lawn mower in a back shed,
D.H. Holmes Christmas boxes in the hallway
for stuffing chicken salad sandwiches in damp towels,
a maroon Pontiac,
a brick house,
a wife who looked like a Creole in a Paul Rubens painting.

Daddy had twelve hairs on his legs.
I counted them and kissed his calves
and held his face and waited in traffic crossing the Mississippi River.
Daddy played checkers and chess and adapted Jack and the Beanstalk with
clip clop clip clop and inheritable sound effects for every story —
we gritted teeth 'cause we loved each other so much.

Daddy made sweet bell peppers and stuffed them with shrimp.
Daddy brought us to hotel conventions and we played pretend with ashtrays
and Bibles and pen pals and pressing elevator buttons.
Daddy had stress and angina pills.

Daddy cried at Ms. Hill's funeral while the small peppery waves of smooth
hair parted on the side made a wavy ramp of hair that plastered him into the
'70s even though he lived till the early '90s.

He died at 59.

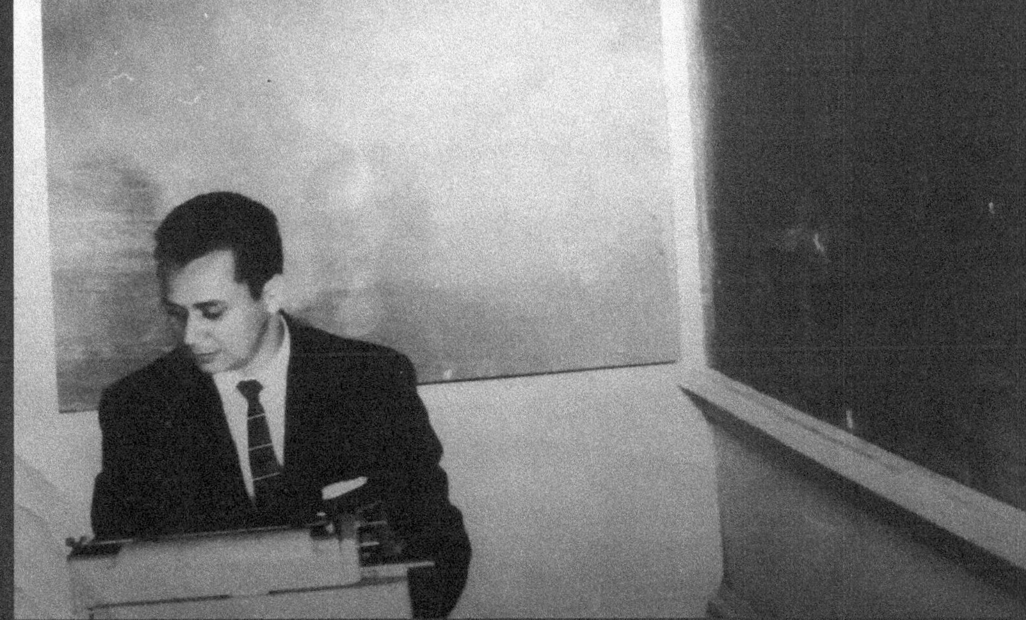

We found him dead on the Elmira St. porch.
That day, mama was in traction, her legs tied up into loops for healing.
She yelped from the phone,
"He's on the porch! They say he's on the porch!"

We zoomed to the scene in our red Toyota Corolla.
He was there. Tossed to the ground. His eyes wide open in death.
Pills clenched in his hand.
Scrambled eggs cooked for his mom's breakfast
still in the brown paper bag.
The sky was grey like it was supposed to be
on the day a good father dies.
It rained.

Somehow, after death,
Daddy walked into the next magnitude
sending me Ray Charles' 'Georgia'
to remember him by,
and many angels to father me.
He wears a vintage tuxedo
in two star appearances,
captivating my dreams.

Mamere Introjection

I. WHILE FRYING SMOKED SAUSAGE I THINK OF MAMERE

My hands hold tight
to the heavy hot handle
of the black pan
I command
smoked sausage
simmering deep in salted sweet butter
each brown little circle of cut meat in grease
introjects ancestral experience
in waves of wondering:

Who was my mamere
Creole and fair?
Pushing up
from the wooden rocking chair
standing above this same pot

her twisted locks of olive-oiled mane
tresses brushed one hundred times
scaring away all of the kink and negro...

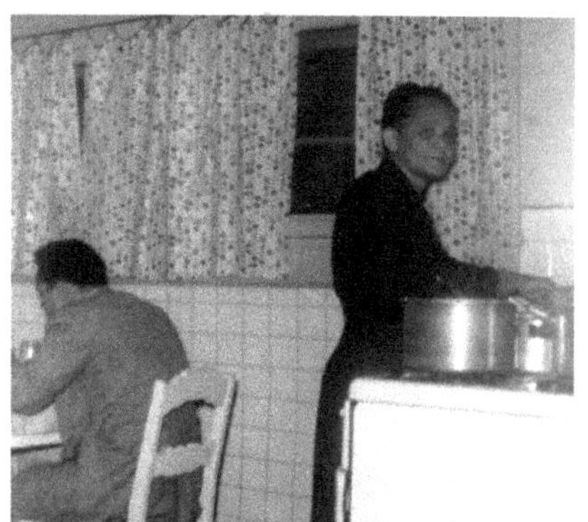

II. MEDITATIONAL HYMN OF 'KINK AND NEGRO' DEEP IN BLOOD AND HAIR

(Say kink and negro softly aloud to the breeze, please
until our motherland ancestors sees, these
holding on tightly to a frying pan if you can)

kink and negro (be gentle)   *kink and negro*   *kink and negro*
kink and negro   *kink and*   *negrooooooo*

stern face
carved throat
bones   adorned in Catholic scapular

I never knew she played the piano until just the other day

Milk of Magnesia trips   to the corner store   Algiers days of yore

III. MAMERE'S GRIEF

Make sure you turn over
each greasy meat circle with the spatula
before they burn

I always go right to Mamere's grief
how she came back
from a trip around the corner to find

                                    the space heater
                                    killing her own mother
                                    in the washroom

                                    flames devouring
                                    the hem of her long silk dress
                                    in a horrific binge of heat

How could Mamere ever be the same
this memory circling around her brain
with the laundry
every time she washed the clothes?

Death and domesticity,
two mean commanders
grief inherited
inside my scowling face

our muscle memory
still rushing great grandma and her burns
crossing the Mississippi River for a hospital
that might treat a colored woman moaning in pain

IV. INHERITANCE

Mamere made us strong descendants of the riverbend
pressing roux into our repertoire
conflict into our character
honing manners into our dinner napkins

She worked hard in a kitchen painted yellow
by her sons and neighbors

her husband in the back shed
sewing mattresses for the socialites of New Orleans
his hands aiding in birthing, bedding, loving,
and praying to God on one's knees

Mamere is somewhere
far further than the pink gown of her funeral

her ample apples
falling from all the mossy trees

I add butter to the onions
I dig the smell of the garlic
and the red of the tomato paste
and plop the buttery smoked sausage
                    doop doop doop in the soup

the greedy grunts of my own husband
glad to eat
and that I cook
a damsel in a dress

I am black and old and gold and wed
and creme and mean and milk and shade
and lickable and angry

I put it all in the pot
I put it all in the pot
and stir it all around

dim and greasy is the stove
dim and greasy is the stove
but the soup is warm
yes, the soup is warm
and the eyes on the walls see me
and the hearts in the home are safe
and the cat is fed
oh, yes, the cat is fed
and the mice are away
from us today.

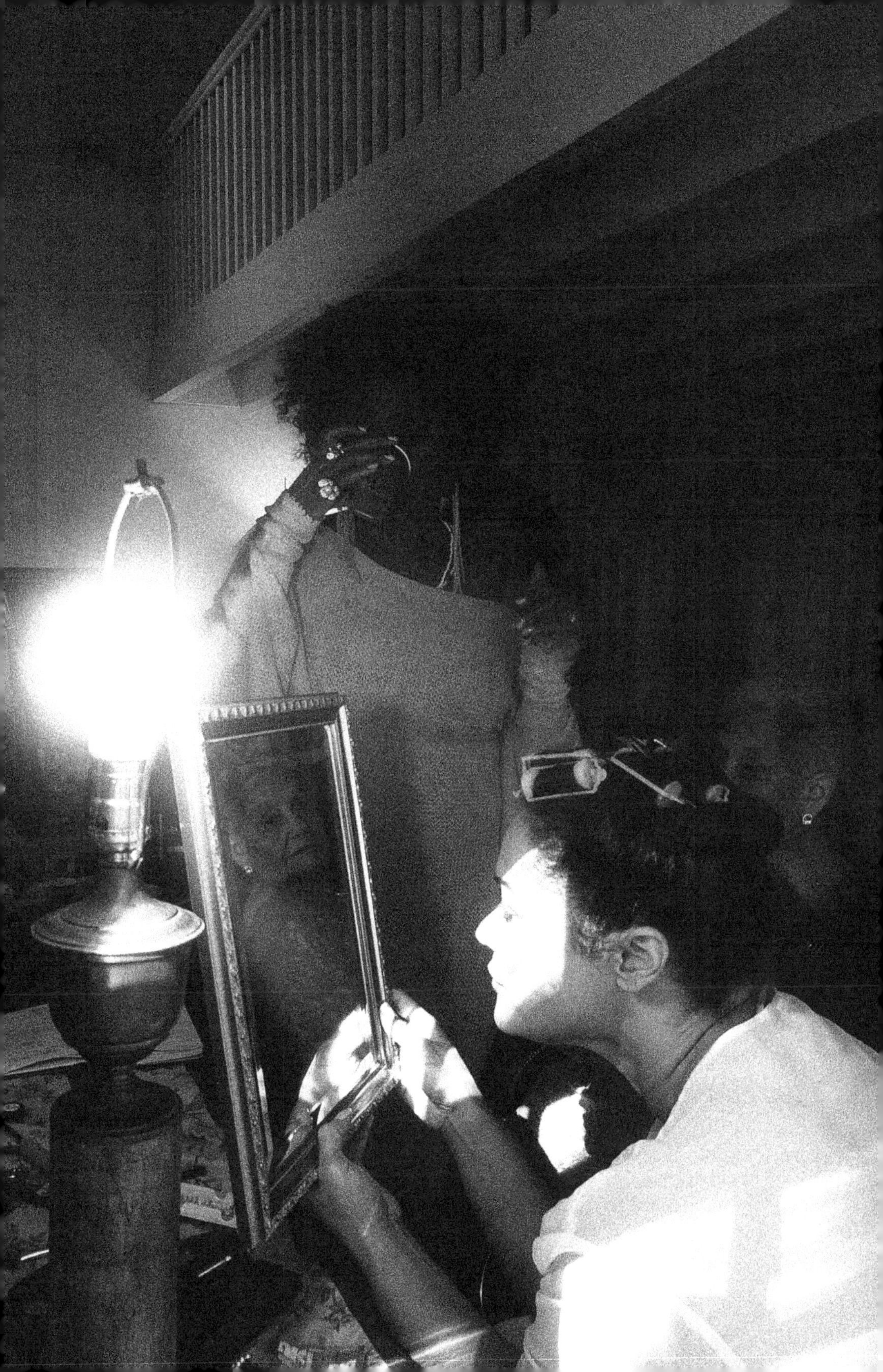

Migration of Mothership Birds

I. THE FEATHERS OF FATHERS

Triumphant triangle of feathers
migrating arrows of mothership birds
directions of family flock

feverish glamour taken by air
flight of fathering femmes

feathers and fathers/feathers and fathers
feathers feathers/feathers fathers/feathers feathers
feathers and fathers/ and feathers and fathers

paternal markings on magnetic beaks
aerial marvels moving towards a better day
flight rhythm rhythm flight

Wayward Warbler   Scarlet Tanager   Indigo Bunting

Swallow   Swallow   Swallow

S   O   N   G

II. AUNTIE GONE NORTH COMES SOUTH

She was the poetry in me
before I knew what a poem was
the female pink pretty part
of my paternal-diurnal-eternal

Auntie was a mystery
to be picked up by the Pontiac
my father, her brother, steering a maroon ship with wheels
quite a prize for a black man taking care of his family
a long car on a slow ride through Algiers

She hopped out the shotgun house
some northern package arrived in style
let loose like an Easter gift in gold stripes and white pants
stunning burst of shot-sugar-candy-style
offered unto the sidewalk

contrasted with the row of gray porches on Elmira Street
and the hardship of slippers shuffling
and the slow moving piggy back rides of mahogany spirits
and the rocks on the road and the brown bare feet

She wore chichi pumps on cracked cement
and smiled the whole way from the screen door to the car door
more cheer than any passerby with a Schwegmann's bag,
she was from the North now —
crisp wisp of weightless never-before-seen ethereal beauty,
a fine feather, a feather, a father

Heart breaker/ heart taker/ bid maker of bridge
seismic sounds of earth passing through one aunt
shopping at J.C. Penney for sales like a wonder

III. GRANDMA'S HOUSE

The house in Algiers she emerged from did its job
containing half-apartment-sized furnishings
for the vital vine in the line — Grand-ma-Mah

Grandma's bed took up most of the second room
each of us would have to walk by sideways
to get to the extremely clean green mop and glow floor
of the kitchen —
the tangerine chairs, the refrigerator of lime green pop
of lime green pop/ of lime green pop
Auntie brought the word 'pop' down south and we wouldn't

S   T   O   P

S   A   Y   I   N   G

P   O   P

A couch of lumps and bedsprings
welcomed Auntie when she visited
each brown sofa pillow with a hole in it
reminding her of where she came from

The north was new with fancy things to do
science and doctors/museums and good moods
cousins with horses you only heard about
boogie black and artsy talk

Welcome back home, Wayward Warbler
jet through the wooden green screen door

a black and white TV buzzing with blurr greets you
black stuck-static panicking lines
try to keep up with the picture

There's the floor I threw a tantrum on one day when I was three
my fists pounding pink linoleum roses
on gray and green fern and frond
the oldest memory of freaking out in front of family
poison for cockroaches kept in caps in the clean corners

The house is a sturdy old man and sometimes a nightcaller
that sends Grandma a-rocking bath and forth
wondering, remembering:

the tales owed to her by history
and the mothers and the aunts and the aunts and the mothers
and the little girls hearing stories about their grandmothers over and over again
and the feathers and the fathers
and the feathers and the feathers
and the fathers and the feathers

IV. GRANDMA'S BATH

I bathed grandma for a time
the wonder of wrinkles in skin
the intimacy of a bath
the keeping-clean-of-a-body
that earned each right to sag/ to lay/ to sway
to slow down and ache
steam escapes the wringing white towel
she lifts up her brown creaky feet from the gravity of the floor
please don't slip in the tub, Grandma
making conversation with the naked body of my ancestry
glad to do it/glad to not have to do it

obligatory meeting- of- rinse
hands move north up an old body with soap
water pours down a musical sink
and the silver tug with a rubber plug
my young spine bends over a large white tub with feet
filled with father and water

father water/ water father/ holy water/ holy father
the feathers/ the father/ the water/ the weather
the pine needles of Christmas time

V. GRANDMA CARRIED A CHRISTMAS TREE ON THE BUS

My grandmother carried a Christmas tree home
for her children on a segregated bus in New Orleans:

Hello, Bus. Hello, Segregated Mode of Transportation.
Hello, Bus. Hello, Slow-moving Long Vehicle of people holding tight to
thoughts and packages and purses and privilege.
Hello, Segregated Bus.
Hello, White People, seated in the front.
Helloooo, Black People, way in the back.
I've got a show for you today.

Please watch my thick brown calves step onto the bus
as I lug a Christmas tree that's taller than me
onto the South Galvez —
its thick prickly bodice of green
poking every arm on the scene.

Don't mind the spiny needles and the jagged tree top
stabbing their way through segregation
all the way to the back of the bus.
I paid my 25 cents, I've been working all day —
cleaning up a house uptown that is not my own.
I wiped up the French bread crumbs, and mopped the floors.
I stacked the towels and did all the chores.
This engine whirring, these bothered stares
this ever-lengthening row of hairspray and blonde hair
the obtusity of the tree is my version of revolutionary.
Nothing is too much to carry for all that you have.
It's smells like Christmas, Mamma's coming home.

Oh, the feathers the fathers/ the feathers the fathers
the feathers the fathers/ the feathers the aunts
and the mothers/and Grandma-mah

VI. THE NEXT TIME YOU SEE ME, YOU'LL KNOW ME

Grandma was the mother of all my fierceness.
All my imaginings were born and reared from
the tea parties in Grandma-Mah's backyard
where she invited our dolls to drink real tea from plastic cups and eat
real strawberry wafer cookies from pretend plates
that posed well as fine china bought at a department store
where she walked browner than her children
and people stared — puzzled by birth and unique choices.

Was she the maid the mother?
the maid the mother/ the maid the mother/ the nanny?
How did she spring these light-colored Italian-looking children into the world
who were black?

They stared at her on the sidewalk of Canal Street
wondering, pondering, judging
just passing thoughts in seconds gone in everybody's life —
how you cross the street just thinking about a piece of cake
or what you need to get in the store
or how and why people look how they look.

In my heart I imagine the people featured in this passed-down story as white,
I admit, in the way we paint cheeky pictures of our distinctions with words
that come easy
and how I came to know from Ms. Georgania and other older gems from
New Orleans that Canal Street was not made for the Negro shopper. Negro.
Ne-e- E-EEE-EEE- EEEE- EEEE- EEEEE eeee EEEEEEE e e-Negro.

And here are the words for birds seeking wisdom from this heirloom-of story:
They stared at Grandma on Canal Street crossing the median
with her children, and she said,
"Well, I guess the next time you see me, you'll know me."

You want to know how many times I've heard that story about
my grandmother in a lifetime?

They stared at us and then your grandma said,
"Well, the next time you'll see me you'll know me."

VII. FURTHER NORTH

Auntie and I would laugh and laugh
cutting our troubles down to half.
She told the story one more time on her deathbed —
after ordering four quiches for her own repast,
calling everyone she loved to say thank you, and goodbye
showing us how to live, to die, to fly.

Wayward Warbler	Scarlet Tanager	Indigo Bunting
Swallow	Swallow	Swallow
S O	N	G

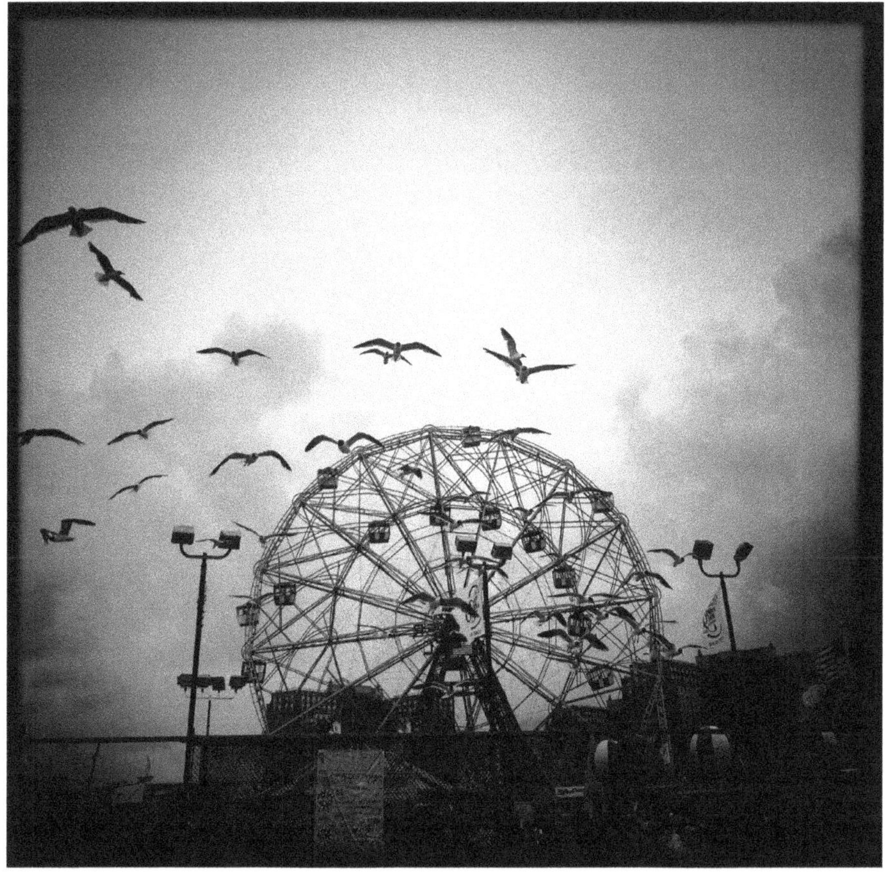

Michael, the Black Cat

Abode
of a good soul
in black fur

Cat king abandoned to a cage.

Rick James of Cat.
Cousin to Aretha Franklin of Cat.
Brother to Juanita.

Royal highness of my own Resurrection.

Counselor for my grieved spirit.

Bastet of Egypt come Mikey of Lenox Avenue in Harlem.

Black paws kneading into my chakras.

Black cat with much booty bending into me for love.

Marking my ankles with his teeth.

Each nip a bloody hieroglyph of possession.
I am his.
I sigh
I sigh
I sigh
I hold his love close by.
Furry one.
Furry son.
Existence in negro.
No words.
Electric.
Breathing God.

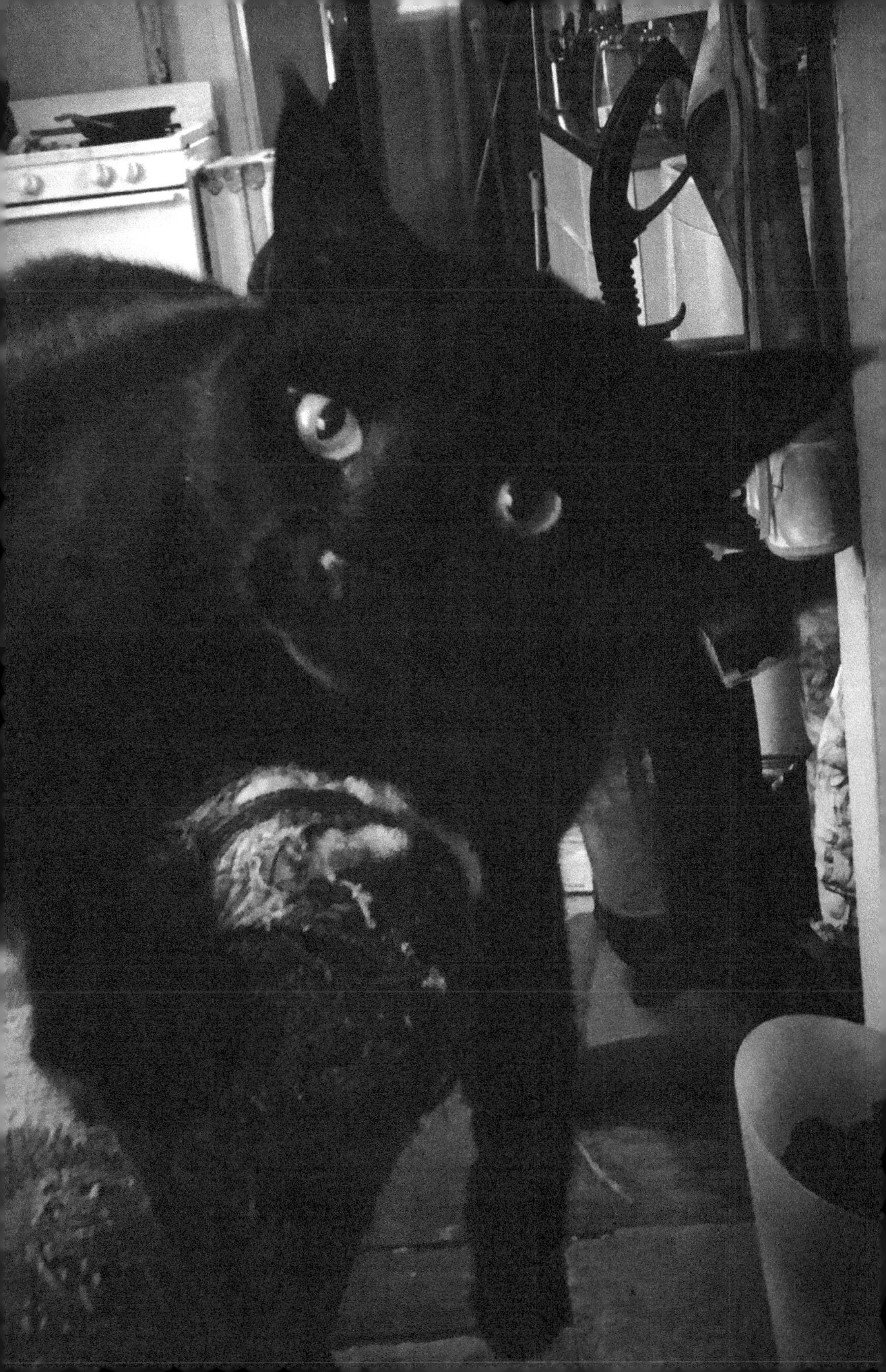

Mississippi Queen of Darkness

Nikki
is black
bird

upside down
fake-feathered memories

cursed cage of feng shui skeletons
Pisces-dreaming-Leo

Nikki
is hair

navy blue river
woven tresses

orange-red
Mississippi mud

copper skin
a blue-bones guitar
begging to be played

Nikki owns
a flapjack friend

quirky
guest-appearing
nomad

who disappears in the grocery store
hospital gown in her purse

Nikki
was kidnapped

by the M3 bus

though her photos
show in Italy

glossy
New York

style and profile
legendary-fake-gold

Raven Chanticleer
connoisseur

lips   legs   tresses

teardrops   hot   dresses

dogs in the yard
brother on the phone
visions shown

hot-pants   generous-chest
heart-pumping   pleasure

godmother of a Black Cat/Diane's girl
                        in
                        the
                        S W I R L

margarita-redbone-treasure

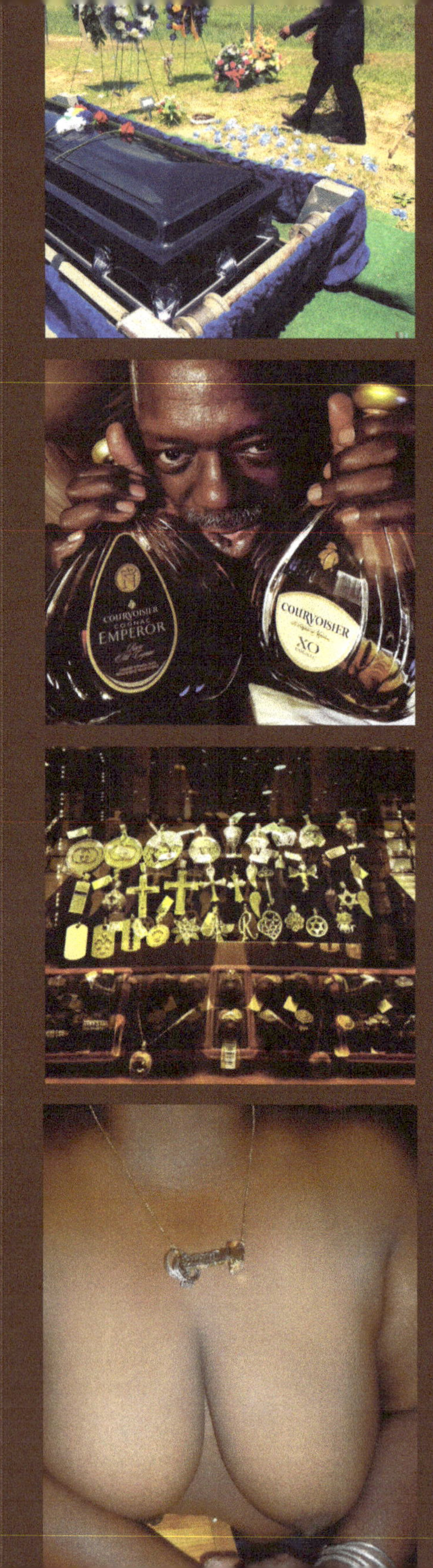

Nikki
knows nighttime

                              parties of vampires
                              teeth rings

                              tits
                              sterling silver clits

the route
of knife wounds

which
organs
get pierced when

                              split skin
                              naked skin
                              rotting skin

is   there

any   dark   thing

Nikki   does   not   know?

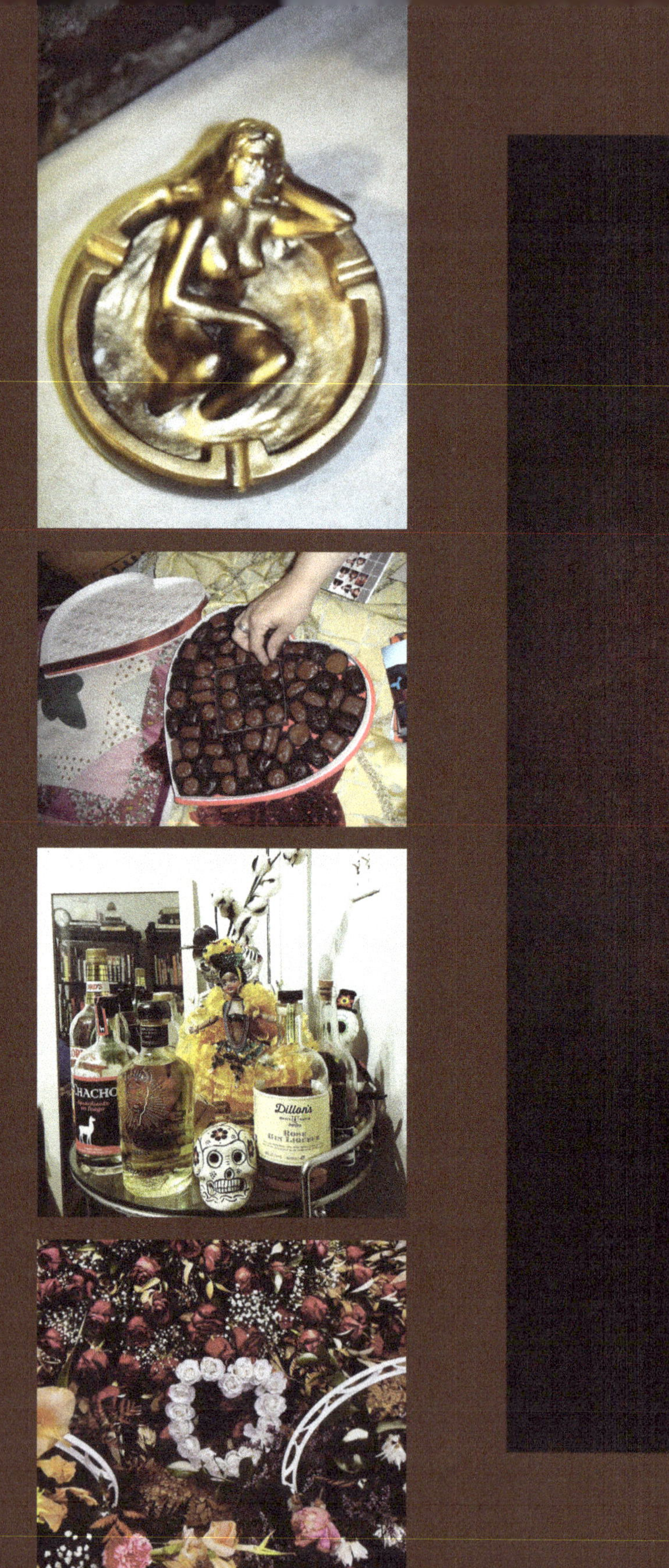

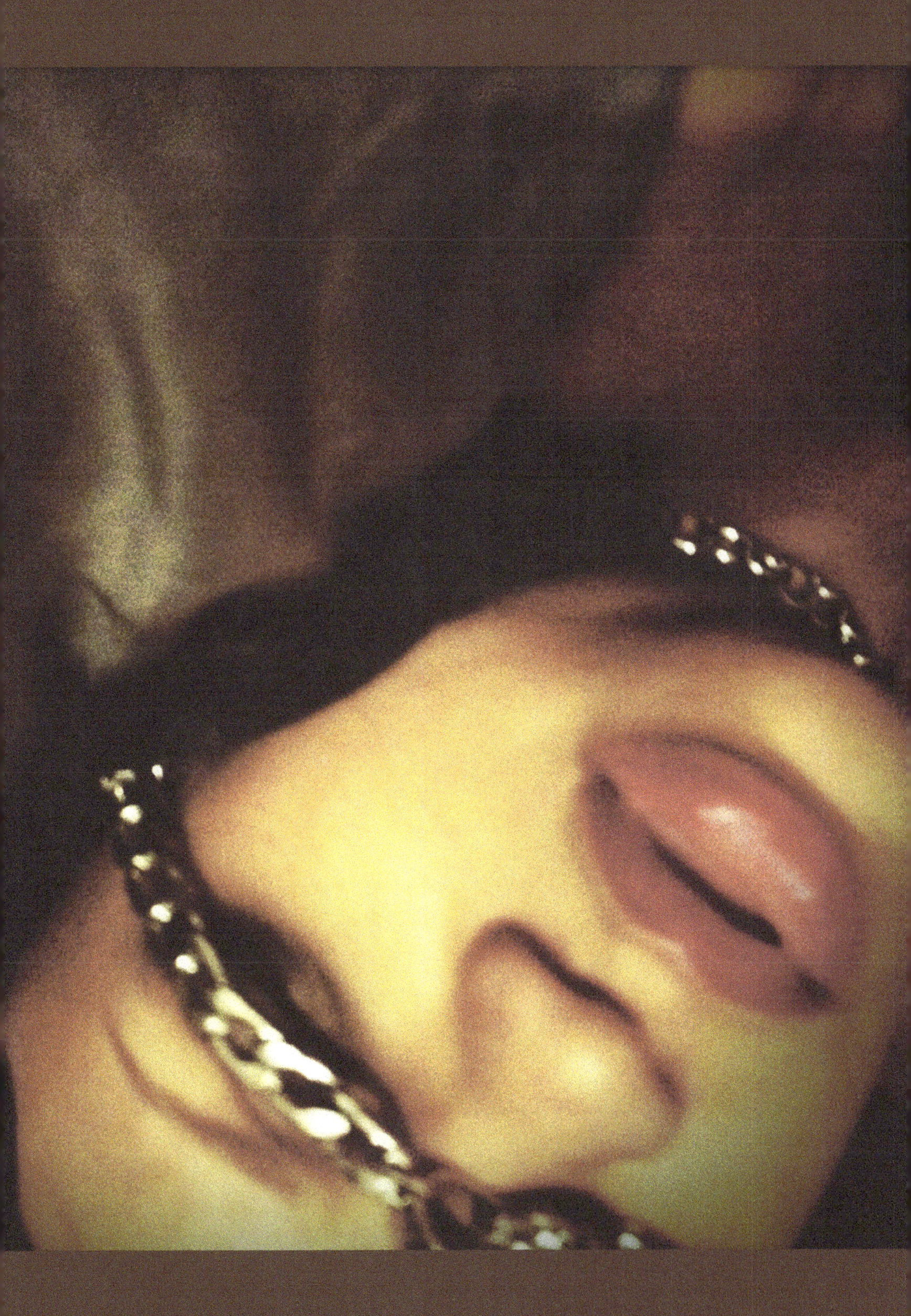

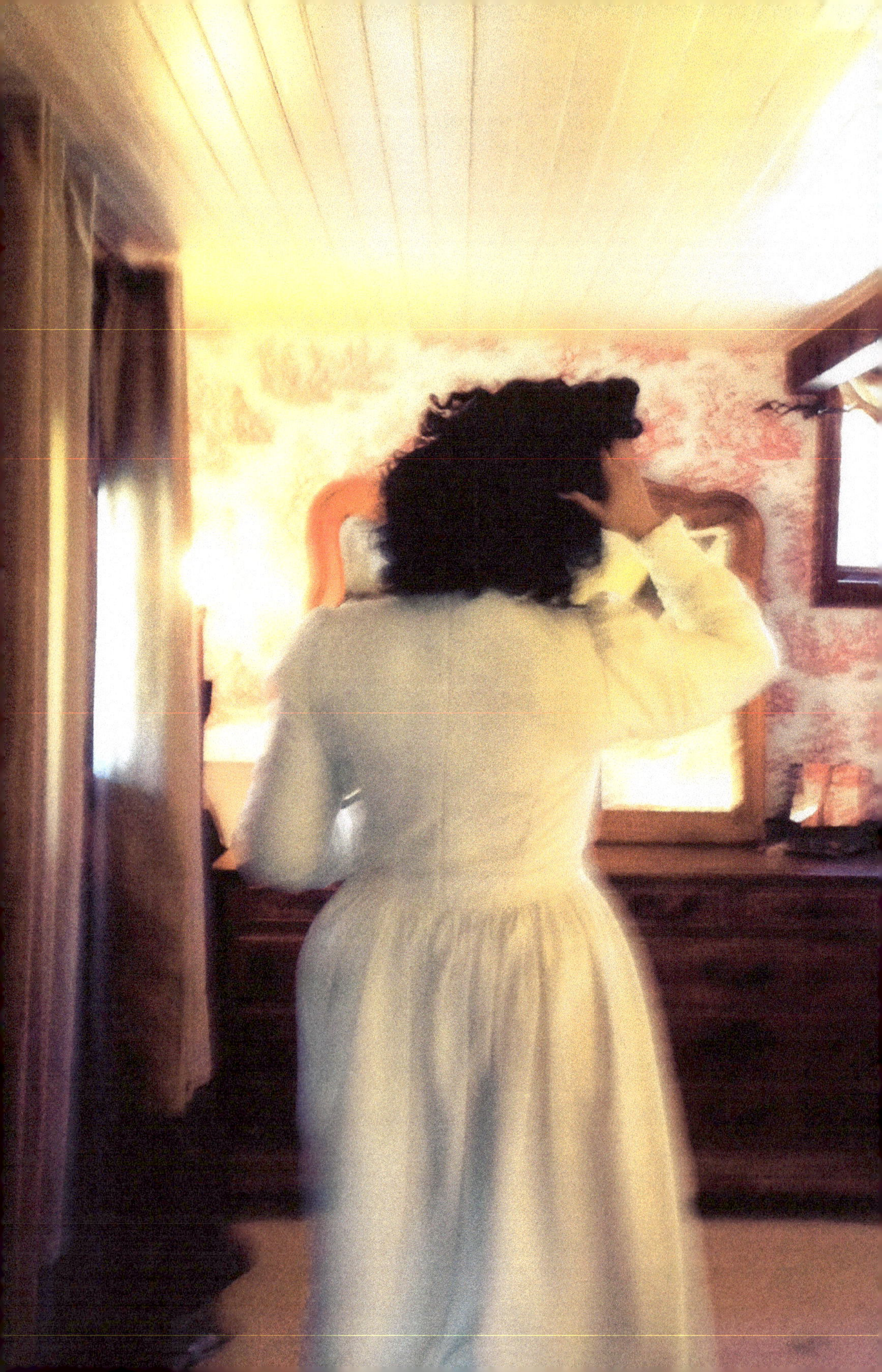

5

GOOD GRAVY AND ONIONS

Naked House

thick cherub cherished
by a cosmonaut of fate

have you ever seen
fat thighs
fat calves
fat belly

embrace a utopia of orgasms?

flying far into weightlessness
my toes missing the scale
instead
they dig into the eternity of a hand-me-down futon

legs   open   on   his   lap

the fire of lift-off beneath a skirt
I've worn in the house
for the past two days

blood reddening my cheeks
both his child and his big woman

fat in his hands   a freak   a spanking   a space station

thine own pelvic tilting with such purpose
making waves for my patch of pleasure

an ergonomic egg chair smothered
with this good gravy of mississippi mushing and pushing

the nerves in my spine are divine
remembering him from another time
karma/dharma/karma/dharma/darling

Husband, husband, come around
so glad the Lord has brought you down
                    and built you here
                    from ash and flesh and memory and mud
                    vocations of scribblings

                              digital pumps of intergalactic space
                              arisen from exquisite doodles
                              on looseleaf paper
                              handsome face/ lips /hips /fingertips
                              rocket ships and futures that emerge from
                              the bones of your fingers
                              curling around the stylus you keep losing
                              a shared parade of scars/ wounds/ prayers
                              a bootlegged red carpet rolls out for us
                              as we continue

more than numbers
more than a green-cash-app of bills
that prefer to arrive way sooner than snail mail

a bomb in my pocket like a docket
another wall to climb
a kingdom come, black man afoot

how can I be this to you so dually?
                                        at once

a warm bath
in a semi-clean tub

wet boats of dust —
lint floating around
both of our bodies

heavy enough
to swell the warm water
into an overflowing gush

the intimacy rich with our wet hands
the legs wrapped and entangled
the green bar of soap/ the dick/ the water/ the suds
the bottom of the tub laughing with squeaks
the handsome there
the flab
the breath
                                        and then

the things we can not share

        the spreadsheet   of days   gone by

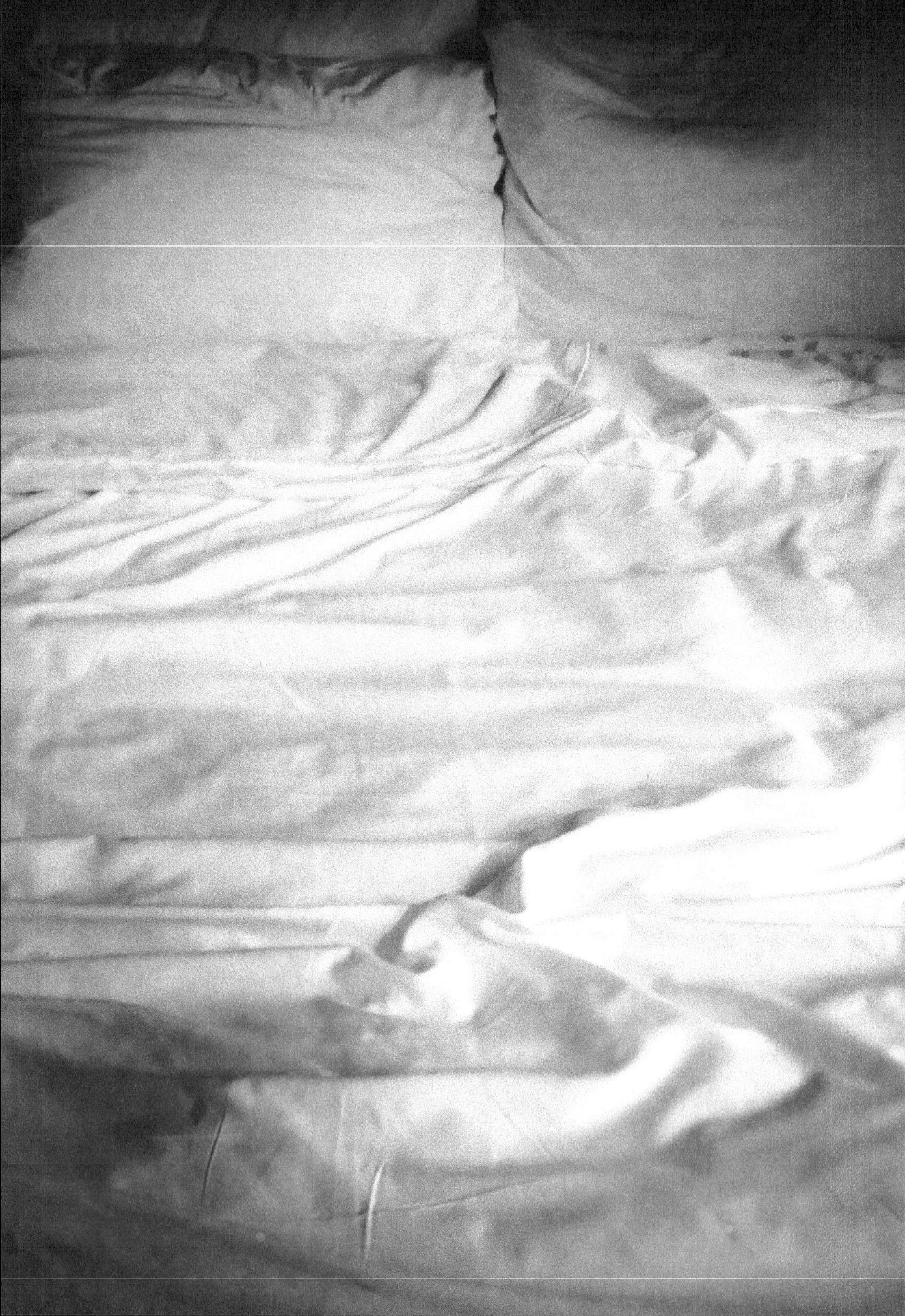

I push the wet hairy patch of all that I am against him

his head belongs to my hands;
he delivers me so many times

my baby   my live recording of God   my afro-cosmonaut in socks

landscape of love
in Harlem pictures

the bowls of gumbo
the stir-fry of whatever we can find

the stank of pussy
left dangling from the love
of a day ago

dust mites
and greasy cabinets

towels torn and old
for us to fold
while we grow old

Rust and Lust

they fucked   to   the   song
being played by the washing machine

                                        the antique box
                                        of rust and lust

twisted the cycle
                    into a beat boxing
                                        romp and bang

twenty minutes thump and pummel themselves by —

clean water
soap
pink socks tangled

                                        corduroys mangled
                                        sweaty legs

the lips
the lid
the lingerie

the rainy day
the folds
the fat
the bones of alone gone

hollow sound
of getting down

Bonding Over Bird Bones

your tongue
waves across my nipple again

I find your eyes
and catch each blinking eternity
given by God
to your eyelash

my fingers taste like garlic sauce

I look across
a table somewhere

the cartilage of bird bones between us
Negroes eating chicken wings for years

you put glitter in my hair
while the toilet we share
says

we live as Lovers in the city

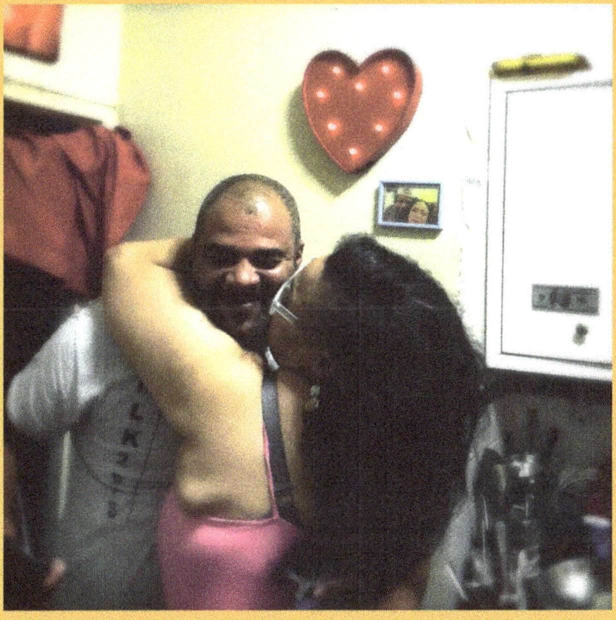

We Real Deal Cool

we fuss-fight
we love-talk
we bite-bitch
we yogurt-walk
we pretzel-play
and live our days
departed from the old ways
of unknown to each other

we yell we yell
we yell
sometimes
We yellow
We bat our eyes too
We link our lips
We yessome
We no and no and no
We eyeball to eyeball
We discuss
We ignore
We bend

We look away
We lift
We lay

Easy

We walk through burgundy mums
sunlight blinding
blanch white light
a bee lands on me

We jump the broom
and fireworks boom
a motley Second Line charges the lawn of the lake.

Did you eat the figs?
Did you have the homemade hot sausage?
Were you there when the kite chugged not-so-far off the ground?
Did you hear the sound
of the entire room singing *Voyage to Atlantis*?
Did you eat the pralines? And warm yourself with homespun mittens?
Did you see the lanterns lit
flames flying far into the starry ghosts of unending time?

I see the whole thing
like the wide view of dimension
driving down Causeway
splitting Lake Pontchartrain with my mama's car

The sky breathes
wide blue messages
of cloudy domes
and patches of storms that pass
I ride through the blue like miracles

Green highways of Mississippi
the ancient lake
traveling down the sidewalks of life
companioning and complaining
figuring out what else to do

BBQ Smooth at the Rodeo

Half-event of being a housewife
watching the horses galloping at the rodeo
silent tongues bite on bitter day
tricks of cowgirls and cowboys mounting designer cattle
the real west
the smokey barbecue
the mountains, beautiful
the yogurt, expensive
the fight, ugly
the chocolate, legally potent cannabis-infused.

She wanted to ride beside her lover
dashing through America's mountains
tanning beneath the sunlight
that found her arm carefree enough to lean from the car window
in a rocky mountain high.

They semi-temporarily-owned that car in the moment.
She wanted to go to the rodeo
the life of a babe, a ride or die
sit on a saddle and rock.

Instead, the car zoomed down a smooth road
nothing from their mouths but silence and frowns
no John Denver
to feel the hallelujah
the mountains so handsome
keeping them from making a joke
or making eyes, calming down,
or singing *Rocky Mountain High* together.

There is the ghost of her
the woman next to him
drawn out like a paper doll
a wife in lines.

She asks for things.
She requires time, a dose of attention that keeps needing to be filled.
She is another cat bowl —
another dirty dish to break in the sink before she threw them all away.

He hears words from her mouth that remind him of too many ghosts she sincerely tries not to be.

She is a mess, a mess with a nest
a broken spine, a face with lines.
She does not bend easily.
She stopped folding the clothes.
She walks up the stairs like she's 70-years-old.

What did it take to raise the vibration that trip?
Red sand, the cabin, the candy-apple red rental car?
Being a Black man in Aspen?
Remembering the foggy dawn they walked across the Golden Gate Bridge?
It certainly wasn't plaid and cattle with tricks.
They were hurt the whole time.

Fancy cowgirls were the only things that strode smoothly
mounted by smiles and waving.
When did they start over then?
When their hosts killed a farm goat they met earlier that evening
and brought him to the table already grilled?
Young people and white girls swooning over him?

She hates driving, but did it anyway.
Realizing he doesn't really want her to carry him anywhere.

Please don't blame her for any questions she may have.
She can't begin to list the trauma figured into losing so many things.
Everything she's lost follows her around
like a train of clanking cans dragging loudly behind her.

He's heard the sound.
His list of losses adds up somewhere that he doesn't tell anyone.
The hurts and balances left undone during the un-fun.
She would like this poem to take a sharp left turn back to love:
the foxiness of phosphorescence, pheromones,
the oxytocin in their brains he referred to

the first time

        his hand

                took hers

                        on the D train.

The Intimate America of Obama Inaugural Day II

Sun goes down on D.C.
peachy-sky
clouds drowsy

plum-colored
fluff

the man I salute
is black and fine
no dazzle
no swearing in

we stand in front of the capitol
creating our own america
just in between our faces

our shoulders touch
shadows sunsets
lint in our pockets
americans

our bellies are blue
pregnant and fat
then empty
with nothing inside

our beds are filled with
stuff we don't need
we roll over pennies mashed to our asses
keeping them like prizes

we charge up our batteries
with cords
and links
and doodles
and sex

and fried fish and grits with the family

we chase wind and busses
                    and trains
                    and patriotism

followed by our wrinkles
we climb up grassy hills
pulling Grand-mamma up and over stone walls,
the links of D.C. chains
rushing to get there,
on the secret winds of CPT TIME

little Soul,
three years old,
wants to wave a flag
so bad,
braids bundled,
bourgeois-broke,
dreadlocks,
Colgate smiles,
jokes about the speakers,
static
five dollar flags
blowing in the wind:

Excuse me:
Dear Obama,
which rhymes with yo mamma, conflama, drama, comma, and Osama
according to all spontaneous raps rhythmically rapped and rhymed
by teens and tweens
walking on the mall after it all
at this historical moment in time —
MLK rhymes with holiday and what you say,
alpha kappa alpha rhymes with my uncle Ralpha:
Dear Obama — we got here, we made it, we've arrived
now ghetto-fried static rips through your smooth
cool black man gentle tone,
like a conspiring cheeky underpaid worker
just slipped off your Inaugural microphone?
static: *zip zip zip* america
gay *blur ba ob khu khu khu* zone...
liberty....Michelle...new do
kuh kuh zz Stonewall...
*d..d..d..*drone...duh... guns...*duh dd..*
Beyonce...*uzzzz* your memorable speech

sounded like *blp bur* gay lib... you..*pblpp..* beee equala... *Kuhzzzzzzz*
too much *hizz fizz* dreaming together,
We will *huzz kuzzah*

As usual, things go imperfectly.
My arms are not Michelle's.
I add just one red dot to the myriad of the masse
who can't even hear your speech, regardless of
our class, our genitals, our desires
standing with my back against the washington monument

america must be here
whispering in my ear
I shed the tear I was supposed to for history,
President Obama,
which rhymes with yo mamma, conflama, drama, comma, and Osama
I'm glad you were there with my family and I
beneath the nostrils of breathing blue sky

sun gone, moon comes,
silhouettes of late night patriots
sitting in washington-worn long johns
smelling like the rank dank stank of collected time and freedom
the politics of
me and my love
figuring out
how to keep
the two of us
in office.

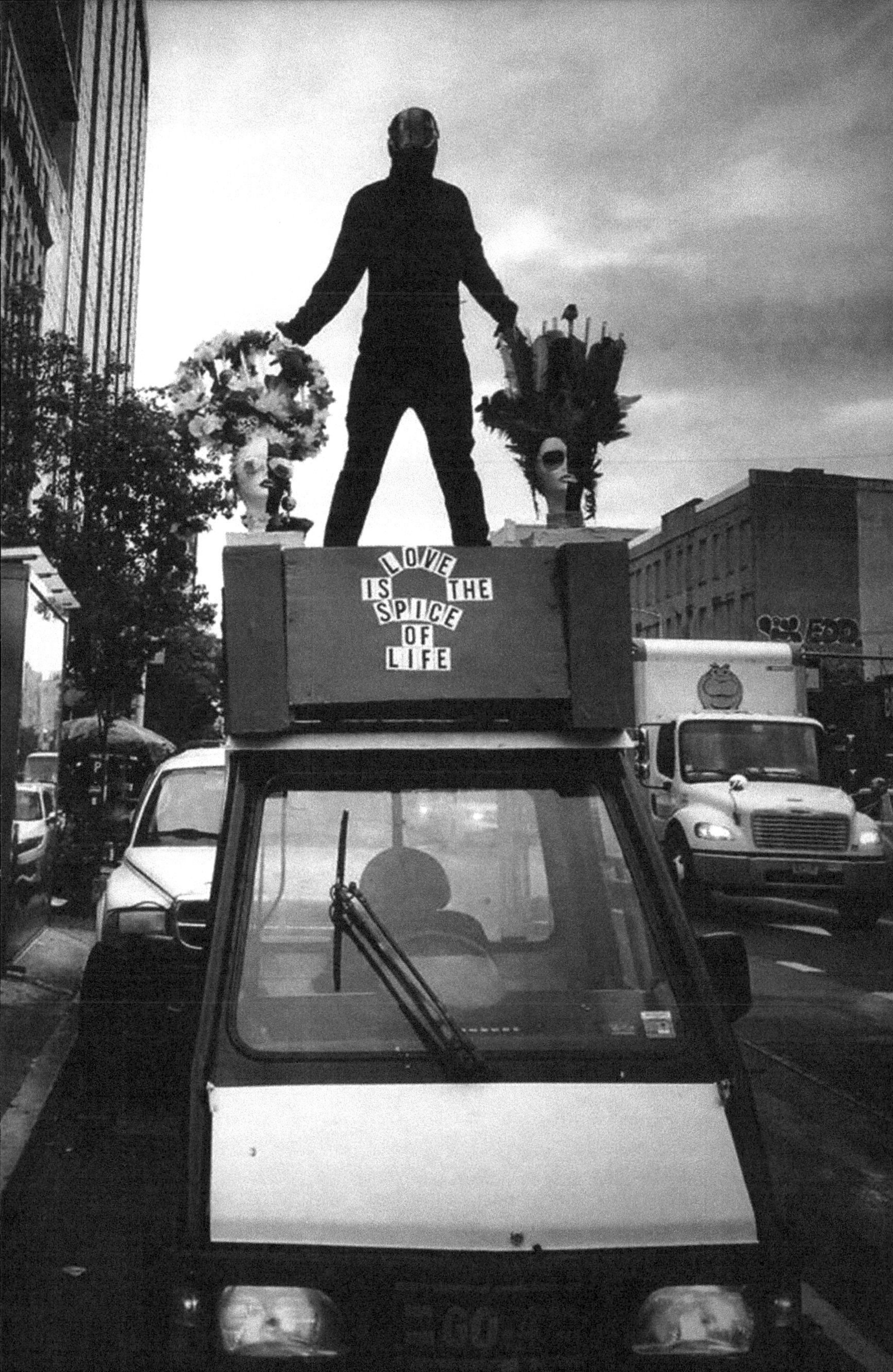

LOVE
IS THE
SPICE
OF
LIFE

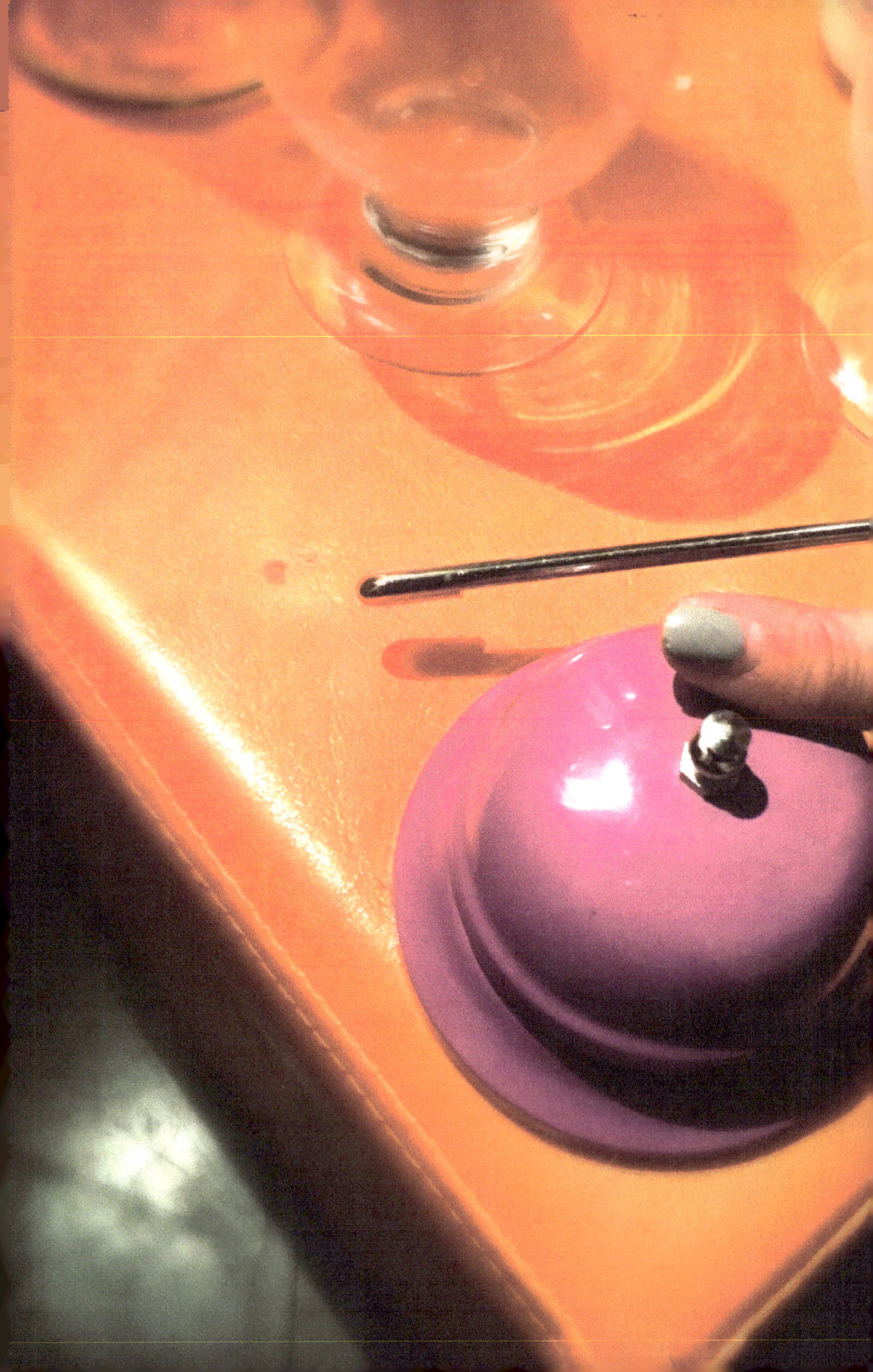

6

GAS VALVES

Gas Valve In My Soul

I am always lonely

and always hungry

an endless hole —

gas valve in my soul.

For Me, It Is the Teeth

I am a caveman
when it comes to this McDouble
this Mac sauce
was lost
till I came
and claimed it
with a club
dragged it to my seat
stuck it in my mouth to eat
ass-spun from the bright red stool

As soon as I'm finished
I blink twice
and rush out the door
licking my lips
swaying my hips
squashing its modicum of respect —
the bright crinkled yellow paper smudged with ketchup
that lands in a can
or stays crumpled in my hand
and makes it to my pocket
for evidence of kill later.

This is true.
A lie is a moo,
I eat that too.

Oh, Hamburger,
I am a caveman
and why don't you have cheese?
This I can demand, please
like any dominating man sees.
Here are the list of things my mouth needs, please heed:

Mayonaissa, grease, gross skin of a chicken-fried,
chocolate with fudge and goo and nuts that becomes my insides
orange, sticky, tight, and sweet,
almonds smothered in vanilla gunk to eat,
Nutter Butters Nutter Butters Nutter Butters Nutter Butters
jalapeno margaritas in succession
hola/ hollah/ hola/ hollah/ hola/ hollah
a Snickers bar, a Snickers bar, a Snickers bar, one more Snickers bar

a lie is a moo
a moo you can chew
a sick brown cow mouth of moo
a moo mouth of untrue
a lie is a moo
a moo you can chew

one Popeye's fried chicken thigh
is the only thing on earth that will never lie
the truth within
its grease and skin
it promises what it delivers
the truth of its crunch
the truth of this lunch

one Popeye's fried chicken thigh
Bourdain-approved can get you high
and even take away grief momentarily
the truth of its crunch
the truth of this lunch
is munch is munch is munch is munch is *much*
Popeye's fried chicken is the truth.

Let's not get lost in the sauce:
these 3 dollars
of sustenance, of means
of capital, of resource
of this gourmand thousand dollar dressing
with relish
is my own devised controlling
of my own destiny
this Butterfinger
this muffin
this small muffin
with poppy seeds
and comfort

each quest
something conquered
and devoured
each quest
I see
I buy
I get

I devour
I devour
I devour with power

Happiness lives within the skin of Popeye's fried chicken
Happiness lives within the skin of Popeye's fried chicken

The dollar is a wrinkled light green passage
a bridge to the other side of want
I push it through the air towards the copper-colored dealer
at the counter standing there,
Middle Eastern flair, the same black shiny hair
I walk across this pact, (intact)
I say it out loud, a deal is made:
the packaging is orange and predictable
easy on the tongue
a far too familiar friend of mine
stately navy blue letters
I've known since trick-or-treat days of old

B–u–tt–e–r–f–i–n–g, see?

B–u–tt–e–r–f–i–n–g, see?

B–u–tt–e–r–f–i–n–g, see?

Who reads the fucking words?
I tear off the package
ripping off the clothes of my new lover
a chocolate bar staring up at me

It's a kill, a kill, a monsterous thrill to kill
the whole bar in three gigantic bites

Mine   Mine   Mine

I am this monster
this loveable monster
not ferocious gorilla
this definitely
hungry
colonizer
a want to capture
to stake a flag where I am.

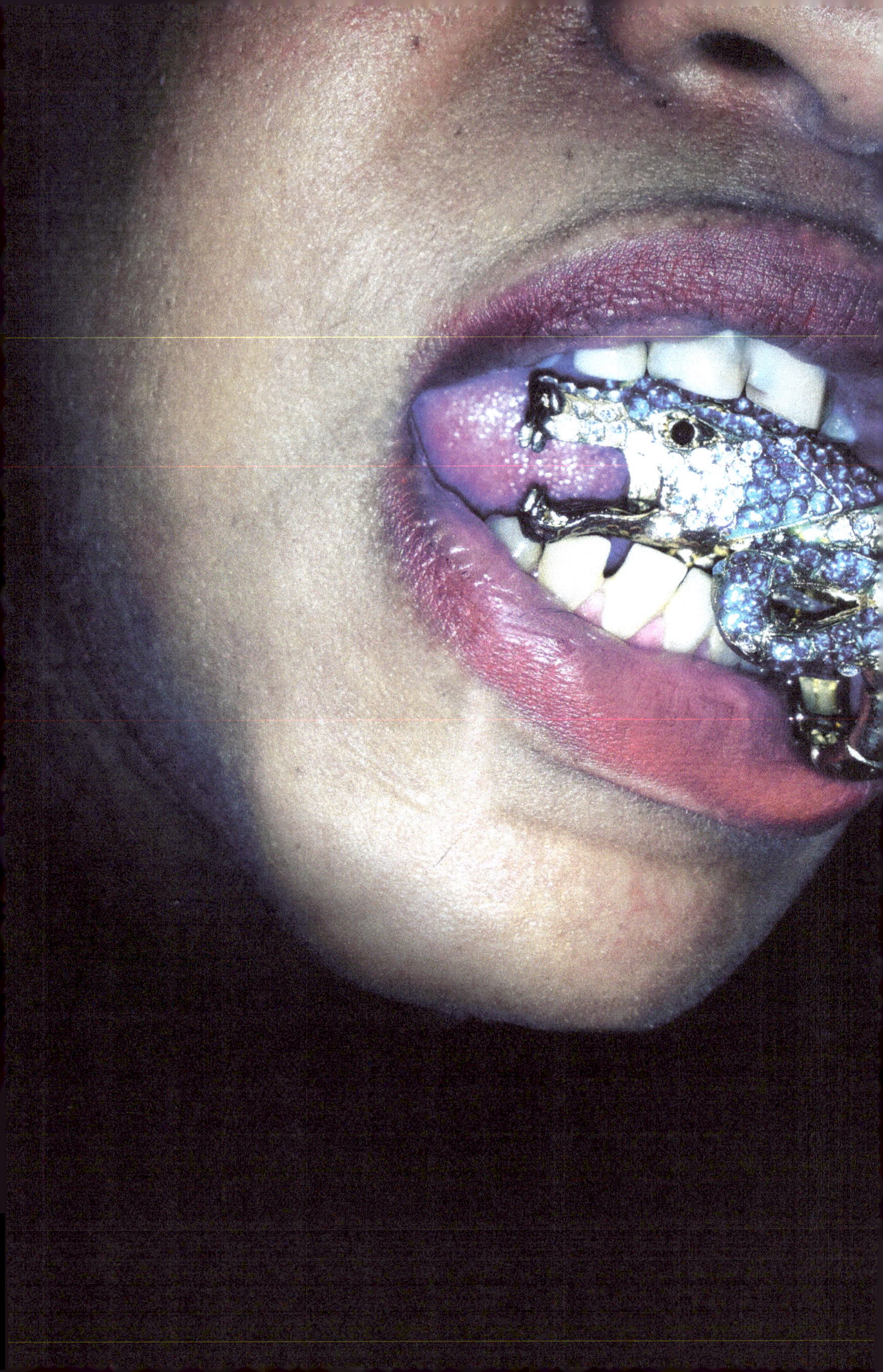

I capture this sandwich.   This tuna melt is mine.   This bacon is with me.

It is not complicated like a relationship.
It is not disappointing like many a day.
It asks nothing of me.
It is meant only to be had
to intertwine con saliva en mi boca
con saliva en mi boca
con saliva en mi boca.
It will never call me rude.
It will never change its mind.
It will never be late.
Upon its arrival,
it seals the deal.
It knows how I feel.

For me, it is the teeth.

The best, the test of the conquest.
The keeping of that thing I have taken in my covetous throat,
long-toothed hoarder of moment and pleasure
getting what I want when I want it, is the treasure to measure.
Icing on my fingers, carrot-cake-thirsty fool, butter to drool.

For me, it is the teeth.

Fireflies, An Easy Birth

It was an easy birth
no fumbling
not too much hard labor
no epidural.

I would say the thought was about a 10 lb. baby born.
Astrologically, Sun and Full Moon in Cancer with a Rising Aquarius.
Slipped right out of me unexpectedly
true to Water-bearing Ascendent,
my own quiet newborn Forgiveness.

It came like Robin Hood
stealing from my own fat
giving back to the part of myself that was starving.
Born in a basement in Brooklyn,
merrymen and matter of fact.

I carried my nursling
out to the backyards of brownstones
to the magical flying lights of dragonflies
the fences of neighbors
Parliament of friend smoking itself away.
I lifted it up to the night like
a black baby born in *Roots*
hailing Brooklyn trees
while freedom was free
and my arms could reach
semi-high into the sky
for a lackluster love
swaddled in tepid liberty
abandoning this bantling
for whatever it is that
comes next.

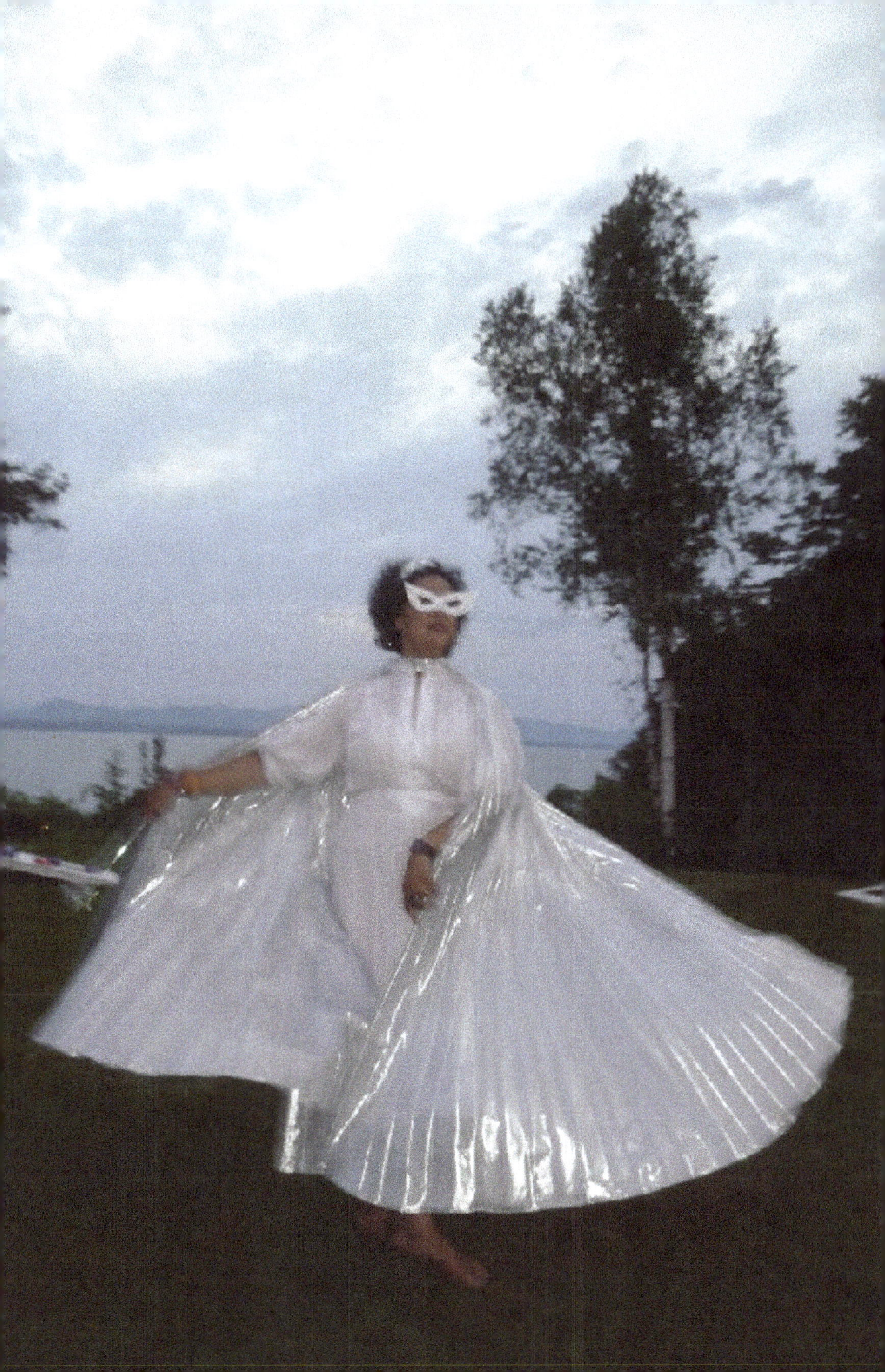

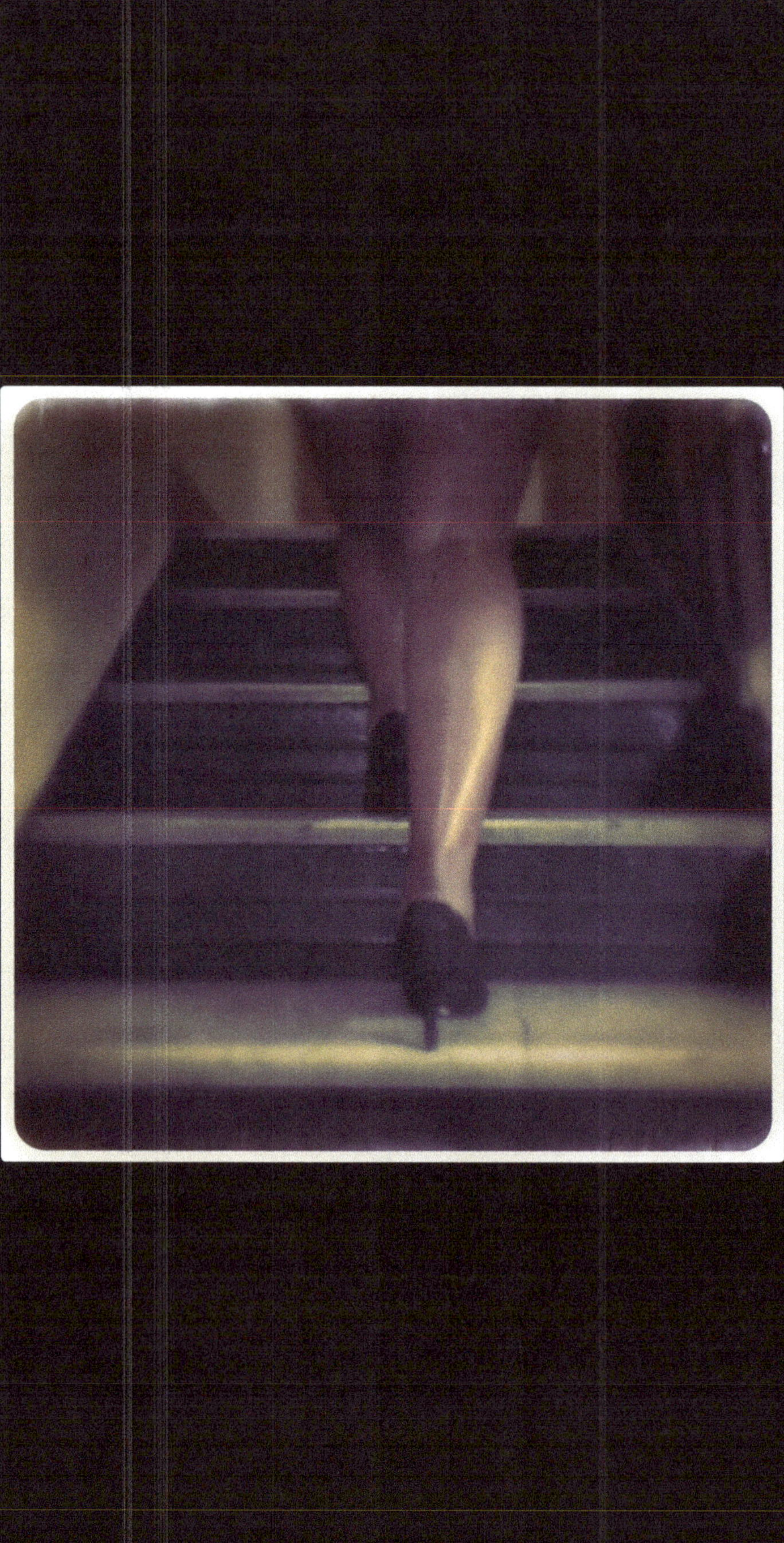

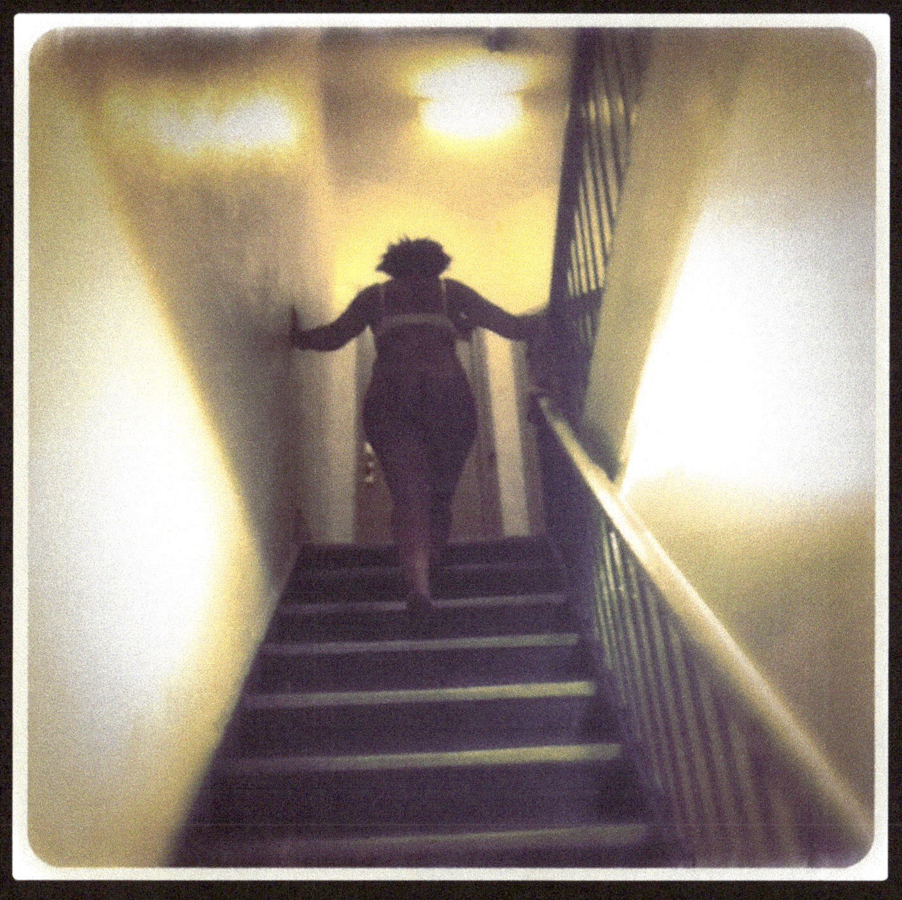

Photography by Nikki Johnson

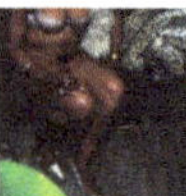
(i)
"Silver Shoes, Harlem" 2018

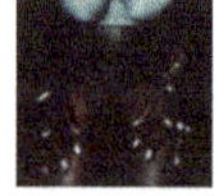
(19)
"The Lady in White" 2018

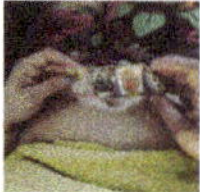
(56)
"Sainted Belly, El Barrio" 2018

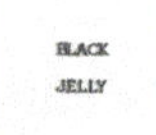
(iii)
"Black Jelly" 2018

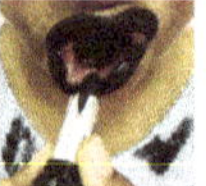
(23)
"Lippy #1" 2018

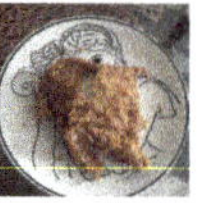
(56)
"Electric Chicken Wings" 2018

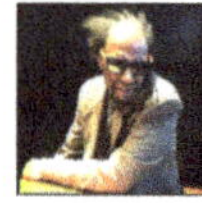
(viii)
"Portrait of Steve Cannon" 2017

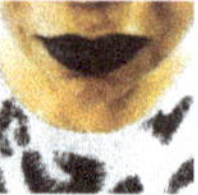
(23)
"Lippy #2" 2018

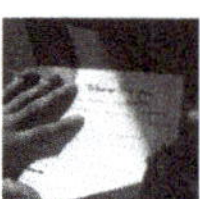
(56) "Words Coming Through, Harlem" 2011

(x)
"Belly Betty, Harlem" 2018

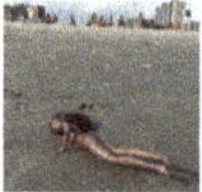
(29)
"Beached, Coney Island 1" 2016

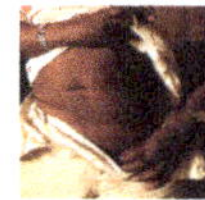
(56)
"Big Jean, Surgical Scar, Bronx" 2017

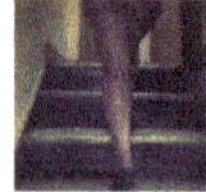
(1) "High Heels Ain't Just for Church" 2018

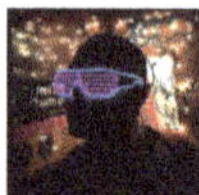
(35)
"M., Lady of Lights" 2018

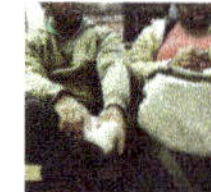
(56)
"Subway Couple"

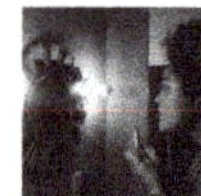
(5) "Mirror Melanie, Vermont" 2011

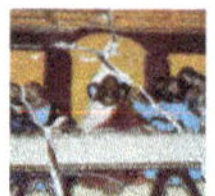
(36)
"Cracked Last Supper, Harlem"

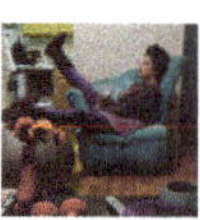
(57)
"5J Lounging"

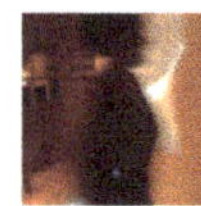
(10)
"Her Shadow, Vermont" 2011

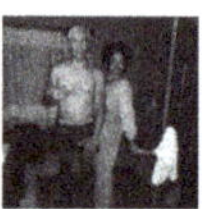
(42)
"Matt and Mel, Vermont" 2011

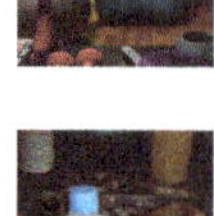
(57)
"Holy Water"

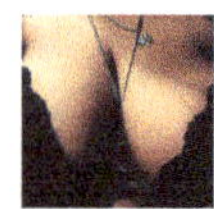
(14)
"Eclipse" 2018

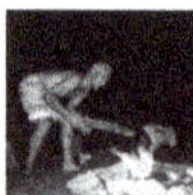
(47)
"Campfire, Vermont" 2011

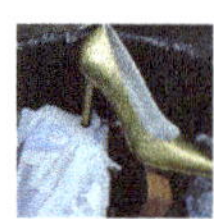
(57)
"Where's The Woman?"

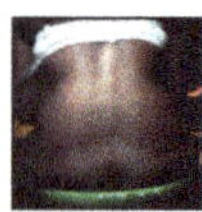
(16)
"Green Seat, Close" 2018

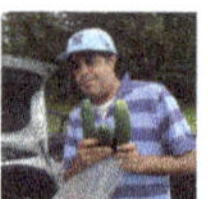
(49) "Charles and his Cucumbers, Vermont" 2011

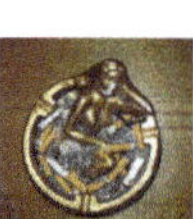
(57)
"Gold Lady, Up All Night" 2006

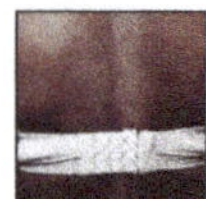
(16)
"Gateway" 2018

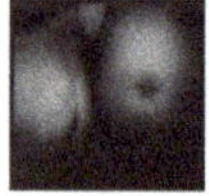
(54)
"Bellies, Harlem" 2018

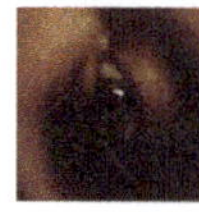
(57)
"Eye, Self-Portrait" 2005

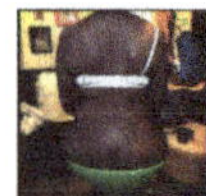
(16)
"Green Seat, Harlem" 2018

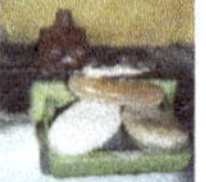
(55)
"Sink, Ave A. Apartment" 2010

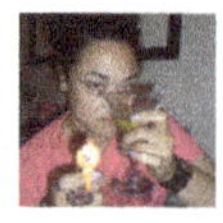
(58)
"Martini at Gunpoint" 2011

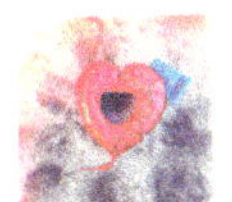 (63) "Caution Heart"

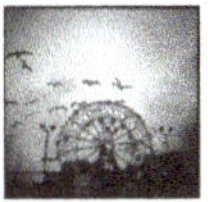 (105) "At the End of the Day" 2018

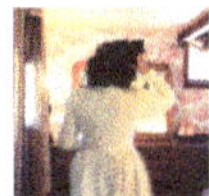 (114) "M. Vermont" 2013

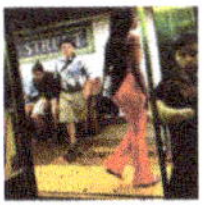 (65) "Miss Red" 2017

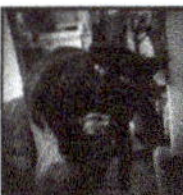 (107) "Mr. Mikey, Harlem" 2018

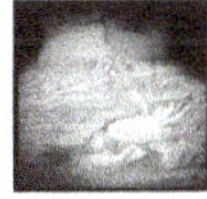 (118) "Sheets"

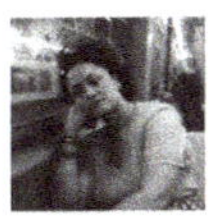 (70) "Subway Blues" 2011

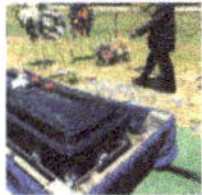 (110) "Goodbye, West Point, Mississippi" 2017

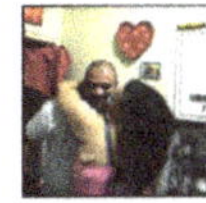 (121) "Kitchen Hearts" 2016

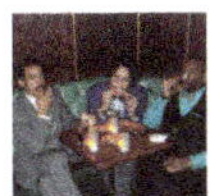 (73) "Lit, East Village" 2018

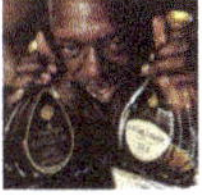 (110) "Big John's Liquor, Bronx" 2017

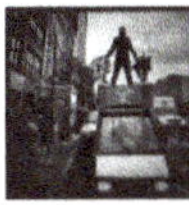 (127) "Love is the Spice of Life" 2017

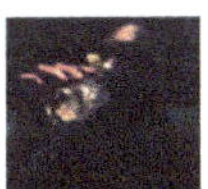 (74) "Sip, East Village" 2018

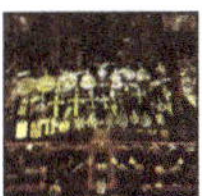 (110) "Gold Shopping, 125th, Harlem"

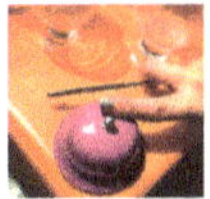 (130) "Bell" 2017

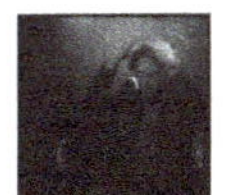 (74) "Men's Room 2" 2018

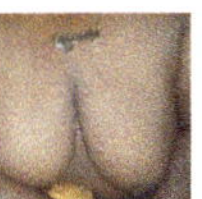 (110) "Jackie, Gold" 2011

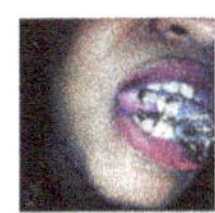 (136) "Dragon Year" 2013

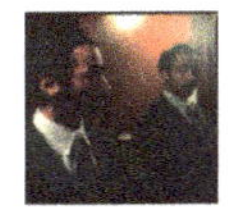 (76) "Men's Room 1" 2018

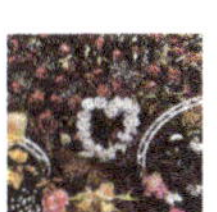 (112) "Dad's Flowers, West Point, Mississippi" 2015

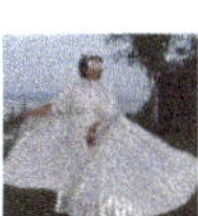 (139) "Birthday Magic, Vermont" 2011

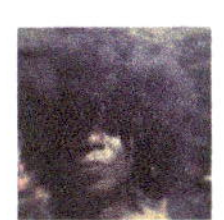 (80) "Day" 2017

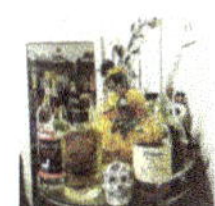 (112) "Home Bar, Harlem" 2018

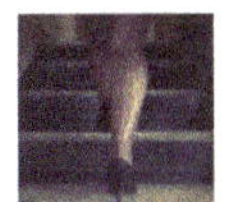 (140) "Level Up, Harlem" 2018

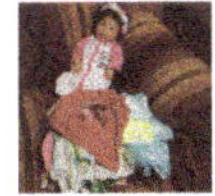 (85) "Gwen's Doll, Mississippi" 2015

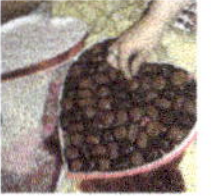 (112) "Daddy's Candy" 2006

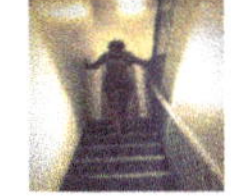 (141) "Ascending, Harlem" 2018

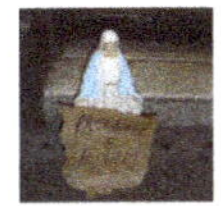 (87) "Homeless Mary, East Village" 2007

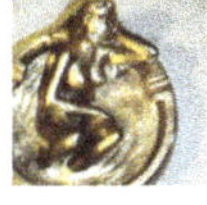 (112) "Gold Lady, All Cleaned Up" 2006

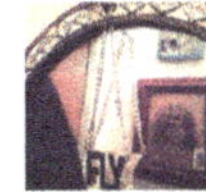 (147) "Fly, Harlem" 2014

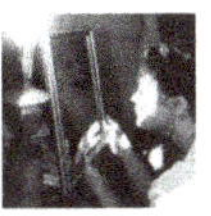 (99) "Wedding Day, Makeup" 2013

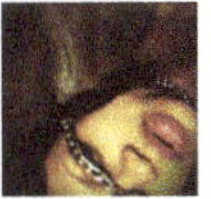 (113) "Bedbound" 2013

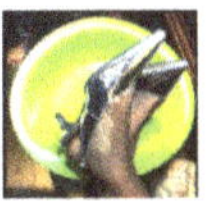 (150) "Silver Shoes, Crossed, Harlem" 2018

MELANIE MARIA GOODREAUX is a poet, playwright, fiction writer, and director-dramatist from New Orleans, Louisiana, living, writing, and creating in New York City. Her work is lyrical, stylistic, unconventional, and many times blends genres for dramatic effect. Pop elements embrace the sensuous, sad, and surreal, while her work addresses the complexities of race and explores the female condition. Southern spiritualism and sex-positive themes find their place together in her experiments with language.

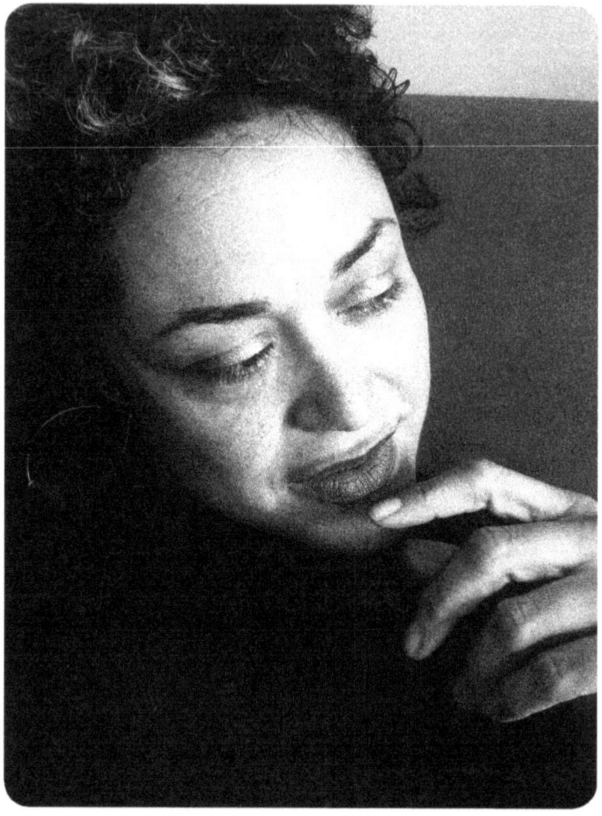

Her work has been published in *WSQ Magazine-The Feminist Press, The Dream Closet, A Gathering of the Tribes #13*, and *Word*. Melanie Maria adapted the lines of thousands of New York City children into the book called *A Poem As Big As New York City*. Her plays *Saydee and Deelores, Walter, Bullets, and Binoculars, Mo'Batz' Ride, Con Trole's Predicament, SWAP, Katrina Who?!, Sometimes It's Very Much About Ownership*, and *Enough Vo5 for the Universe*, have been featured at Chelsea Playhouse, the House of Tribes Theater, the Abingdon Theater, Studio Players Theater, the Linhart Theater, the Lillian Theater in Los Angeles, the Nuyorican Poets Café, HOWL Fest, the New York Theater Festival, the Hudson Guild Theater, and Theater for the New City.

She teaches creative writing and drama in New York City while living in Harlem with her Afro-futurist husband, the illustrator, Tim Fielder.

NIKKI JOHNSON has exhibited her portraits and documentary photographs widely in the United States, Europe, and Asia. Her photographs depict situations that are alternately inspiring and despairing. This Mississippi-born

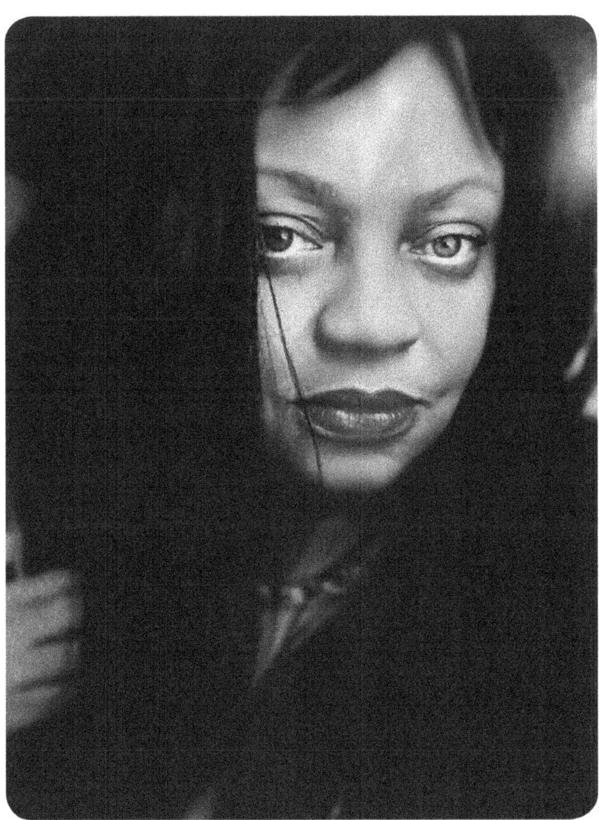

artist creates visions that reflect economic disparities; victims of urban malaise lulled into serene contemplation, and cluttered shelves in homes with contents that yield revelations about their owners. These photographs are loaded with details — portraits of compelling people surrounded by unusual, ironic, even humorous, elements. The results of these exchanges between photographer and subject are a collection of exotic documentary, portraiture, and still-life images that embody urban and rural collisions, coded objects, and social explosions. Her images formalize the coincidental.

Johnson holds an MFA in photography from Rochester Institute of Technology as well as a BFA degree from Mississippi University for Women. She was the first photographer ever admitted to Henry Street Settlement's Artist in Residence program, and was a participant in *Fictive Days*, a Berlin art residency. *The New York Times* art critic Holland Cotter described her photographs in the show *"Back to Haunt the Hell out of You"* as "disturbing and moving." She is also currently half of the collaborative duo *Death Under Glass*, a project that reveals the artistic merits of images created by microscope during death investigation.

Her photographs have been published in *Art in America, DIF Magazine, Time Out New York, HYCIDE,* and *Hustler* magazine. She has published two books with Mäekask Editions, *Natural History* (2010) and *We Buy Gold* (2013).

Nikki Johnson currently lives in Harlem, New York.

Acknowledgments

There are many people who have helped to birth this book — readers, designers, models, friends, poets, my family, and my wonderfully supportive husband. Immense gratitude goes to Julia Brennan, David Andrew Stoler, Elizabeth Koster, Michele Lanclos-Eli, Michael Chenevert, Anthony Harper, Jonathan Duran, Caroline Snape, Diane Sullivan, Makita Gilliam, Mark Holloway, David Kahl, Bruce Morrow, Jeffrey Rosales, Matthew Thorsen, Janice A. Lowe, Tim Fielder, Mikey the Cat, Don Eggert, Frank Esposito, Monica Goodreaux, Carmelite Goodreaux, Shelly Eversley, Shawn Lipenski, Major Jackson, John Jennings, Tracie Morris, Anthony Tee Saralegui, Gene Alexander Peters, Keith Roach, T. Scott Lilly, Albert Iturregui-Elias, Kimberlyn Leary, Lucille Leary, Charles Drew, Dorothea Smartt, Liza Jessie Peterson, Mariposa Fernandez, Melisol Fernandez, Kathryn Dickinson, Lytza Colon, Bob Borsodi and Jimmy, Steve Cannon, Lois Elaine Griffith, Jacqueline Dowd, Clark Gayton, Maryam Myika Day, Sidney Goodreaux, Sheila Maldonado, Raven Chanticleer, Sara Jane Munford, the little girl who created the compelling image of being a jar of black jelly in a costume one summer at Theater Camp, Cindy Hanson, Stephanie Bok of Write Night at Frank's, Pirl and Connie Johnson, Rickye and Mirta Johnson, Big John, Bikram Yoga Harlem, Theater for the New City, The Langston Hughes House, White Bird Productions, A Gathering of the Tribes, and God.

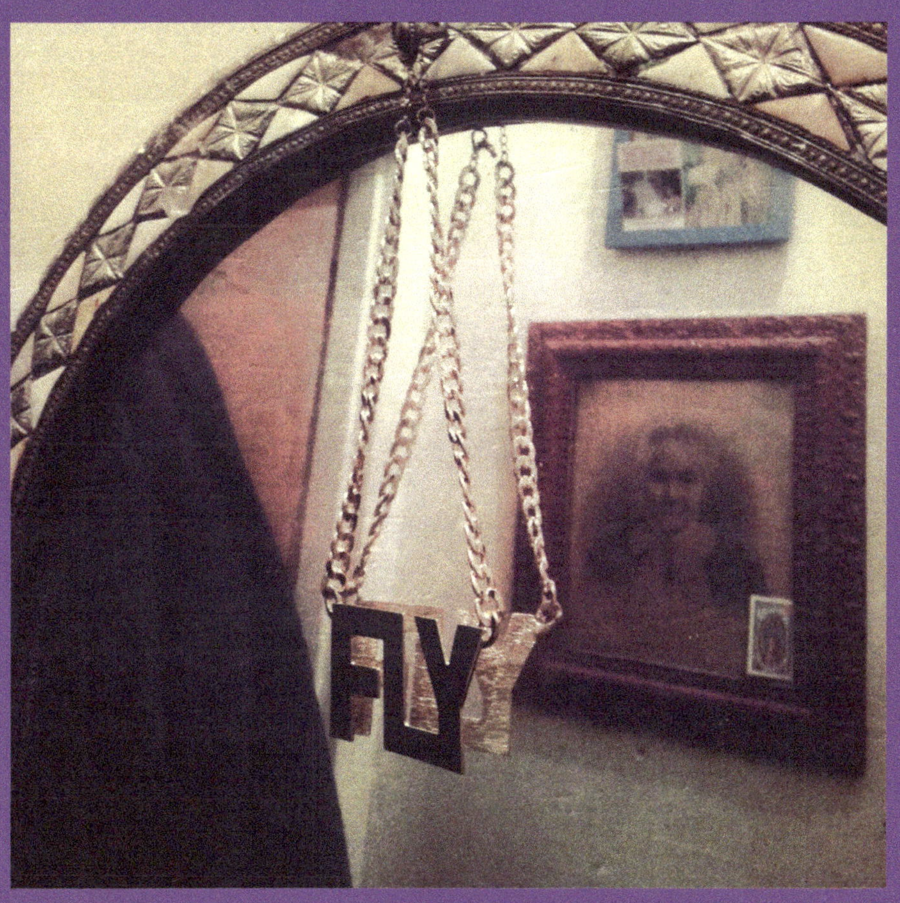

"If you pay attention to us, you will never grieve."

THE ANCESTORS

"Everything in the world changes
and nothing is ever gone."

REVEREND DIANE SULLIVAN

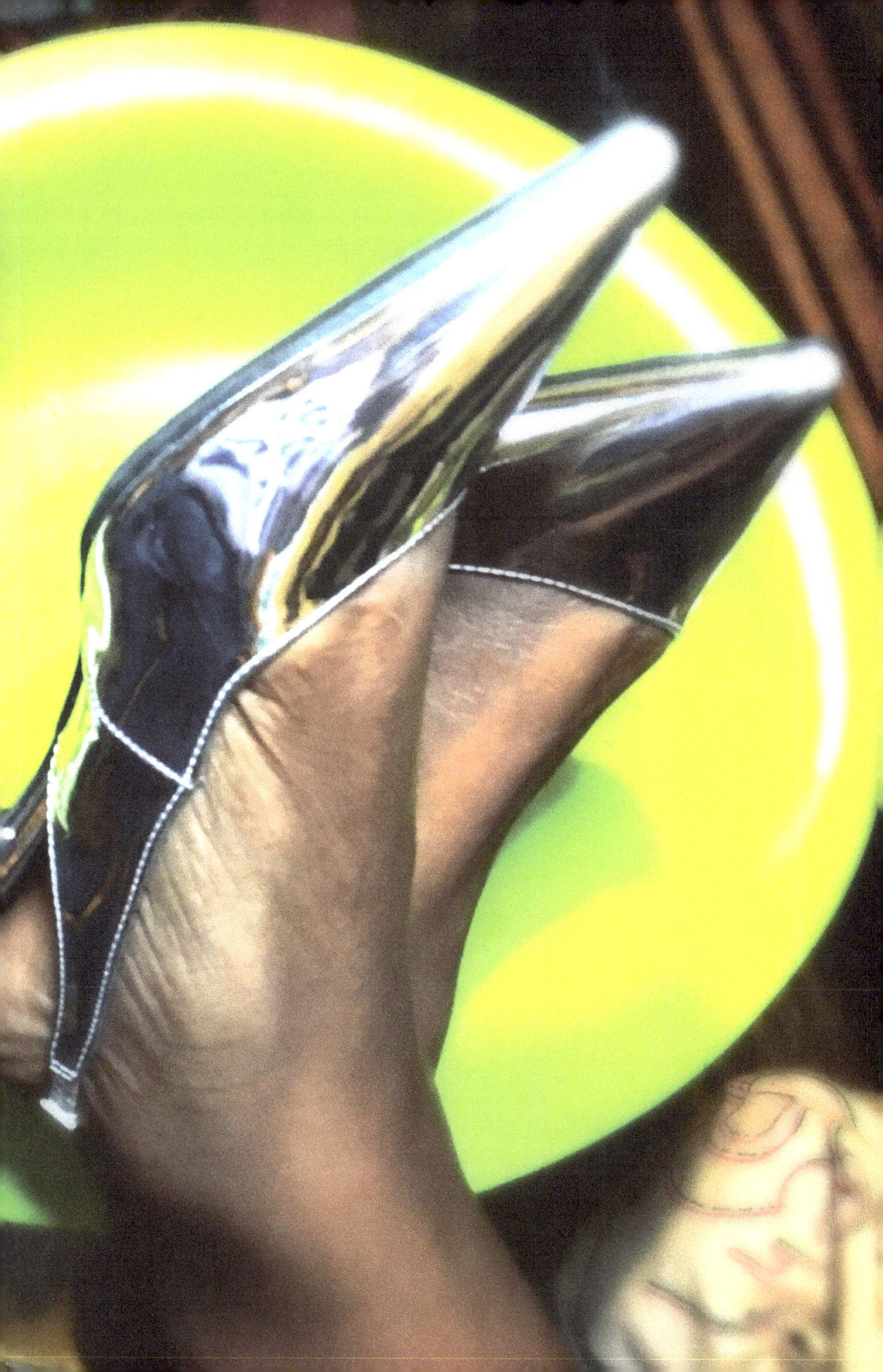